PRAISE FOR BOOKS B

"Heady stuff."

— *School Library Journal*

"Carlson explains science in terms that teens can understand."

— *Voice of Youth Advocates*

"Carlson writes with intelligence, spunk, and wit."

— *The New York Times Book Review*

"Practical focus on psychological survival skills."

— *Publishers Weekly*

"Dale Carlson has written over fifty books, and she is deeply committed to opening up young minds."

—*The Book Reader*

The Teen Brain Book: Who & What Are You?

"*The Teen Brain Book* will help teenagers understand why the teens are so tough and terrifying, why their parents and other adult figures seem against them. It also provides a look at the least understood part of the human body, an examination of the functions of the different parts of the brain, the effects the brain has on our lives, and ways to rewire one's own brain when it causes pain and suffering. *The Teen Brain Book* also serves as a compilation of the ideas of many of the world's leading scientists on the brain and human existence."

— Eric Fox, 18, Teen Editorial Director

MORE PRAISE

Who Said What? Philosophy Quotes for Teens

"Evocative, thought-provoking compilation and very highly recommended reading for teens and young adults."

— *The Midwest Book Review*

"With her introductory remarks and selected quotes, Carlson invites the reader to meditate on a subject and make a personal judgment as to its meaning."

— *Voice of Youth Advocates*

"A superb reference…could help student to see the world though many sets of eyes. The author encourages the reader to see the diversity of philosophies and to use this to form one's own philosophy…a good addition to any junior high or high school library."

— *Lorgnette of Texas*

"In a time of such world conflict…it is natural to seek to understand the nature of other people…to find common ground in the hope of ending misunderstanding…*Who Said What?* has located the common threads of Eastern and Western thought, old thought and new, and compiled them into one work….This book encourages those who live only in conformity not to give in."

— Eric Fox, 17, Teen Editorial Director

MORE PRAISE

In and Out of Your Mind: Teen Science, Human Bites
New York Public Library Best Books List 2003

"Contemplating the connectivity of the universe, atoms, physics, and other scientific wonders...human beings and their biology, philosophies...ethics...a thought-provoking guide...into the mysteries of outer and inner space in an approachable way...drawings are informational, humorous."

— *School Library Journal*

"Carlson explains science...and challenges her readers to make them think about the environment, humankind's place in the world, and how ordinary people can...change things."

— *Voice of Youth Advocates*

Stop the Pain: Teen Meditations
New York Public Library Best Books List 2000

"Much good advice is contained in these pages."

— *School Library Journal*

MORE PRAISE

Where's Your Head? Psychology for Teenagers
Christopher Book Award
New York Public Library Best Books List 2000

"Psychological survival skills...covers theories of human behavior, emotional development, mental illnesses and treatment."

— *Publishers Weekly*

Girls Are Equal Too: The Teenage Girl's How-to-Survive Book
ALA Notable Book

"Clearly documented approach to cultural sexism."

— *School Library Journal*

The Teen Brain Book

Who & What Are You?

THE TEEN BRAIN BOOK
Who & What Are You?

DALE CARLSON

Edited by Nancy Teasdale, B.S. Physics
Pictures by Carol Nicklaus

BICK PUBLISHING HOUSE   2004   MADISON, CT

Edited by Director Editorial Ann Maurer
Senior Science Editor Nancy Teasdale B.S. Physics
Book Design by Jennifer A. Payne, Words by Jen
Cover Design by Greg Sammons

www.bickpubhouse.com

Library of Congress Cataloging-in-Publication Data

Carlson, Dale Bick
    The teen brain book : who and what are you? / Dale Carlson ; edited by
Nancy Teasdale ; pictures by Carol Nicklaus
        p. cm.
    Includes bibliographical references and index.
    Contents: Who am I? What am I? Am I? -- What do I do with my life? --
What's your story? -- Am I really free? -- Am I unique, or like everyone else?
-- Brains and behavior -- Human beings are wounded -- Why we behave as
we do -- Evolutionary psychology -- Sociobiology, social psychology -- Neuroscience -- The effect of intelligence on your conditioning -- Tools for change.
    ISBN: 1-884158-29-3
    1. Neuropsychology -- Juvenile literature. 2. Brain -- Juvenile literature.
3. Cognition -- Juvenile literature. 4. Teenagers -- Juvenile literature. [1. Neu-
ropsychology. 2. Brain. 3. Psychology. 4. Cognitive psychology. 5.
Adolescence.] I. Teasdale, Nancy. II. Nicklaus, Carol, ill. III. Title.

QP360.C347 2003
153--dc21   2003050001

Available through:
Baker & Taylor Books
Bookworld Services, Inc. Tel: (800) 444-2524 Fax: (800) 777-2525
Quality Books Tel: (800) 323-4241 Fax: (815) 732-4499
Ingram Book Company
or: Bick Publishing House
307 Neck Road, Madison, CT 06443
Tel: (203) 245-0073 Fax: (203) 245-5990

Printed by McNaughton & Gunn, Inc. USA

Dedicated to the two medical mentors of my life

My father Edgar M. Bick, M.D., Orthopaedic Surgeon

and

My daughter Hannah Bick Carlson, M.A. Developmental
Psychology, M.Ed., Counseling Psychology, C.R.C.

With infinite love and gratitude
for giving me life and purpose

.

Books by Dale Carlson

TEEN FICTION:
The Mountain of Truth
The Human Apes
Triple Boy
Baby Needs Shoes
Call Me Amanda
Charlie the Hero

TEEN NONFICTION:
Who Said What? Philosophy Quotes for Teens
In and Out of Your Mind: Teen Science, Human Bites
Stop the Pain: Teen Meditations
Where's Your Head?: Psychology for Teenagers
Girls Are Equal Too: The Teenage Girl's How-to-Survive Book

ADULT NONFICTION:
Stop the Pain: Adult Meditations
Confessions of a Brain-Impaired Writer

with HANNAH CARLSON
Living with Disabilities: 6-Volume Basic
    Manuals for Friends of the Disabled

with IRENE RUTH
Wildlife Care for Birds and Mammals: 7-Volume Basic Manuals
    Wildlife Rehabilitation Series
First Aid for Wildlife

■

Acknowledgments

To the great, and my personal favorites, philosopher/scientists and philosophy/science writers of this century: Daniel C. Dennett; Stephen Jay Gould; J. Krishnamurti; Stephen W. Hawking; Steven Pinker.

To R.E. Mark Lee, Director of Krishnamurti Publications of America, and editor of *The Book of Life: Daily Reflections with Krishnamurti*.

To Ann Maurer for ten years of steadfast support, guidance, and insight as Editorial Director of Bick Publishing House.

To Eric Fox, Teen Editorial Director, for his bright mind and right comments.

To Anna Brewster Smith, high school teacher, who devoted hours of precious time to reading and commenting on this manuscript.

and

To Hannah Carlson, M. Ed., CRC, for her work with developmental disabilities and mental illness, and her books *Living with Disabilities* and *I Have a Friend with Mental Illness* from which she permitted me to borrow generously.

■

CONTENTS

Foreword

Introduction

SECTION ONE
MIND-BRAIN: HOW WE WORK

■

SECTION TWO
HUMAN NATURE: HOW WE GOT THIS WAY

.

SECTION THREE
BRAINS AND BEHAVIOR:
THE SCIENCE OF CHANGE

.

FOREWORD

The brain and the mind are two different things not easily understood by philosophers, scientists, or even brain researchers. How the brain works is actually the subject of most all the books on psychiatry, psychology, philosophy, sociology, history, economics, and all of the arts of life including drama, poetry, fine arts, and music. All of our lives, all self-expression, and all of literature is really about one issue: "Who am I?"

Dale Carlson has presented the complex world of the brain, science and mystery, in a way that teens and non-scientific people can understand. This is no small task either to undertake or to accomplish. By the time you finish reading this book you will discover that no expert, philosopher, or scientist can give you an answer to the question that is asked on the first page of this book and that human beings have been asking for more than five thousand years: "Don't you suffer?" It is left to you to discover the answer and that is done by a most simple and direct looking within.

Without the use of obtuse, scientific jargon, *The Teen Brain Book: Who and What Are You?* holds up a mirror so that teens can see directly how the brain works and how experts from many fields debate the mirror. I am always two-minded about books about the brain, being overawed by the subject and unsure as to whether it can be understood by anyone. But Carlson gives you the key to understanding your brain, which she shows is already in your hands.

R.E. Mark Lee, Executive Director
Krishnamurti Foundation of America

INTRODUCTION

The human brain is an extraordinarily powerful tool for survival and pleasure and accomplishment. It is an equally extraordinarily powerful instrument for causing pain.

There is an old saying: keep your friends close—but keep your enemies even closer. This is so you can observe and understand their every move before you get hurt.

We need to treat our brains in the same way, keeping an objective eye on them at all times, paying attention to them so they behave in ways that neither hurt ourselves nor other people. Few people have been taught the way to do this; even fewer have figured out their own brains for themselves. So the human race, while its brains build marvelous technology, still suffers after tens of thousands of years, from violence to others and brutality towards itself.

Don't you suffer? Aren't you tired of it?

This is not a self-help book. This is a book of science and philosophy about the brain and how it works, particularly about and for teens. It is easy to understand and to use, to help figure yourself and other people out because, more or less, and whether in English or Chinese, all human brains work the same way. There is still a lot we do not know about the secrets of the brain's functioning. But what there is to know, teens should know before they make the same mistakes as adults that the whole human race has been perpetuating since it began.

Dale Carlson

SECTION ONE

Mind-Brain: How We Work

CHAPTER ONE

Who Am I? What Am I? Am I?
The Brain's Best Kept Secret—How It Creates a Self

Do you ever have the feeling that your own brain is trying to drive you mad? That your brain is in conflict all the time, that it drives you into dangerous activities or relationships? That it wrecks your sanity by falling in love; makes you follow strange, even dangerous, urges; pushes you to the edge by telling you awful things about yourself, the world, what's under the bed?

The brain, the way your brain produces your self and your brain's capacity to change that self, is the subject of this book.

MIND-BRAIN: HOW WE WORK

Who and What Are You? Even, Are You?

The answer to the question "Who am I?" is easy. It's your name, if you knock on a door and you are asked who you are. It's your name, your age, your grade in school, maybe whether you are male or female on a school form. You add an address and telephone number if you make a new friend, or if the police stop you for speeding. That's *who* you are. No problem.

"What am I?" as a person is harder to answer. And it is far more important. What you are is what you are thinking, feeling, your attitudes, your behaviors. All that is the sum of your *self*. All that is what you are. And that self, the sum of your thoughts and memories, affects not only you but everyone else. If what you are is nasty some days, you give off nastiness. If what you are some days is full of sharing and good will, what you give off is really nice. It follows then that if your brain is full of crazy feelings and thoughts, what you give off, what your self, your personality gives off, is craziness. It's the brain's thoughts and feelings we must pay attention to.

We're not talking about necessary technical thought, remembering your name or your internet password or chemistry formulas, or to run if a truck is after you. We're talking about the suffering caused by the chattering of psychological thought. Is your brain so full of psychological thoughts and feelings that you'll do, listen to, buy into anything to turn off that inner racket, that sense of being a rat in your own maze? Welcome to the world of the human brain—especially the teen brain.

WHO AM I? WHAT AM I? AM I?

Everybody thinks. Everybody thinks all day, everywhere, all the time. It's what the human brain does, in thousands of languages, in billions of heads, all ages, all sexes, all colors, under all kinds of hair. Baby, teen, and grandma, rich stars and the homeless on the streets, girl or boy, professor or prisoner, we all share this common human-specific activity. We think. As cognitive scientist Steven Pinker says in *How the Mind Works*, "natural selection is a homogenizing force within a species....That is why all normal people have the same physical organs, and...the same mental organs as well." If you think about that, about how everybody's brain is doing exactly the same thing as yours, you'll never feel unconnected again. Especially since all those mental organs, all those human brains, are pretty much doing all that thinking about the same subject: myself. All animals are aware and can communicate. We humans, however, have more than awareness of our surroundings to keep us alive. And more than communication, humans have speech, and so, thought. Both neuroscientists and philosophers tell us that thought, based on memory, creates the idea of a self.

This, naturally, brings up the third question: after *Who am I?* and *What am I?* comes *Am I?*

It seems to many important scientists, like philosopher and neuroscientist Dr. Daniel Dennett, that if you look down inside your shirt, you won't find anybody. Or, as he says in *Consciousness Explained*, "the trouble with brains, it seems, is that when you look in them, you discover that there's *nobody home*. No part of the brain is the thinker that does the thinking or the feeler that does the feeling." The 'self,' it seems, is an invention of thought, a story that a person's memories put together. (I have noticed for myself that if I stop thinking because my attention is on a movie or a book or a person I love, the 'I' of me seems to disappear. There is then the feeling of having to pull my 'self' together again, as if pieces of my self were scattered everywhere in my brain. Have you had this experience?) And no MRI or PET scan has yet located an actual, physical 'self' anywhere in any brain. We are back to the tricks of psychological thought.

We are finally beginning to understand how we think. Yet still, no one knows why we think. The mystery of human consciousness remains unsolved. Mind/brain science, with all its neuroscientists, evolutionary biologists and psychologists, behavioral geneticists, artificial intelligence engineers, and all the philosophers of consciousness—no one has yet understood entirely the mind part of the human brain. We are beginning to understand thought. But our human brain has two main capacities: it not only thinks, but it observes that thinking. We have both "intellect and intelligence, which are not the same thing," as the world teacher and philosopher J. Krishnamurti says in his book for teens, *What Are You Doing with Your Life?* Intellect is thought, knowledge; intelligence is understanding what to do with that knowledge.

Part of the problem in understanding the mind/brain is that, while thought is physical and mind needs the physical brain to function, mind that connects with god, the universe, whatever you like to call it, mind that produces joy and happiness, not just pleasure—this *mind* cannot be, says neuroscientist Dr. Richard Restak, "reduced to a formula, involving brain circuits or chemicals."

But it is not mind-intelligence-insight that drives us crazy. This, in fact, may be what saves us. It is intellect with its knowledge and thought, the chatter of thought, that torments us, and causes inner violence (rage at self or others) and outer violence (taking that rage out on others).

What Is Thought and Thinking?

Yet most of us, even though we are thinking all the time, don't even ask ourselves: what is thinking? Isn't thinking, the process of thinking, a response to memory? Memories, experiences, personal and genetic, from something your mother said five minutes ago to evolutionary information received five million years ago, are recorded in the brain and are expressed as thoughts and feelings, opinions, judgements: in short, your self. As neuroscientist Joseph LeDoux puts it, "life is change," and "the brain records those changes." After all, the main business of the brain is to keep the body alive. The brain is our primary organ, the control center for all the body's voluntary and involuntary activities. The brain is physical. What it does is physical. *Thought is physical.* It is based on speech produced from memory recorded and stored in the brain. Thought, and its creation, the self, are the past. Observation, insight are needed to face life now.

We know this is so: what we don't know, although there are hundreds of theories, is how thought happens. Is it our genes that wire our brains to think and chatter all the time? Is it our personal experience? And what for? Is thought a warning? A cure? Helpful, or just crazy-making, like a tic?

The human brain, with its brilliant accomplishments (Alexander the Great had begun his conquest of most of the known world barely out of his teens, and Mozart, by thirteen, had already written concertos, sonatas, and symphonies), its terrifying disorders (Alexander was obsessive, Mozart manic-depressive and alcoholic), its complex circuitry, its relationship to its own body, to other brains, to the world—especially to *itself*—remains an unexplained frontier. The brain feels so lonely that we can't seem to understand others. We can't even seem to understand ourselves entirely. Partly, this is because we don't know how to look at ourselves. Partly, it's because the brain has a hard time looking at itself except fuzzily in the mirror of other people's reflection of us and our words and behavior. One great value of relationship is that we can use relationship to see ourselves and what we are in the reactions of friends, family, teachers, therapists, peers, as well as in our reactions to them.

Human mental complexity, human thought, needs to be understood so we can stop suffering and passing that suffering on to other people. We can use one of our brain's capacities, intelligence/observation, to examine the other capacity, thought. And we need to understand, not just escape our pain—not because understanding is virtuous, but because escape doesn't work for very long. Escape doesn't work because it causes more pain. It is *seeing* that dissolves psychological pain.

Too many people, instead of trying to understand what thought is and how to handle its psychological confusion, shut out the racket with drugs, too much television, busyness, loud noise, falling in love, people or food addictions, shopping, sports—any distraction they can find. Then, of course, we get stuck with the consequences, like going broke or getting fat. It's easier on the system in the long run not to escape, but to recognize thinking, mind chatter, as a human brain activity and deal with it. We'll examine tools for doing this in later chapters.

Because while science, philosophy, and religion have not yet understood the entire mystery of human consciousness, we have figured out various pieces of it. One day we'll fit them all together; until then, understanding the pieces will help. And if you can find a new piece of the puzzle, or can reinterpret an old piece, tell all and help the rest of us out.

Understanding the teen brain, and the developing complexities of its struggle into adult maturity, may be the key. Most ten-year-olds in our culture are not yet driven off-balance by hormones: they know without much confusion what they want, from a new toy to adult or peer approval, and how to get it, and they've gotten pretty good at being a kid after ten years. Teen hormones, sex, and the teen brain's need to fight for independence against parents who often don't want to let go, changes all that. Teens live in conflict and confusion, a kind of shame at still needing parents, a kind of guilty pleasure when they don't.

The problem is that while the teen brain is still producing lots of new cells, it has still not completed its wiring, its neural circuitry, especially in the frontal lobes, the prefrontal cortex just behind the forehead, where judgement takes place. When you were a child, your parents, sometimes your teachers, told you what to do, what not to do, and acted as your frontal lobes; now your brain is developing its own judgement circuits. This creates conflict, but it also gives you a new responsibility. You, not just your parents, teachers, the society around you, are in charge of shaping your life, your thoughts, your self. These neural connections, however, are not set in cement, and what you choose to do or not do, whether to live constructively or destructively, be part of the world actively or watch television passively, all of this will be wired into your brain circuits and affect the rest of your life.

Understanding the teen brain will help us comprehend all human agendas, what personal, biological, and cultural conditioning has gone into the wiring of our brains' circuitry. We must understand our own conditioning, the mistakes the human brain has made historically in cognition, in its thinking patterns, and what we can do to change whatever in our brains is destroying us individually and collectively. It may be true that there is a decrease in the production of new brain cells as we grow older. But the rewiring of connective material goes on all our lives long, allowing us to change our behavior and our attitudes until we die. And to survive—change we must!

We must pay particular attention to the effect of intelligence on past conditioning, intelligence being a whole different quality than memory, than thought chattering away. We must see human potential, not just accept that what we have done is what we must continue to do. Our biology is not our destiny, as evolutionary scientist Dr. Stephen Jay Gould points out in *The Mismeasure of Man*.

This brain science book for teens affirms that it is possible for each person to alter her or his wiring—by observing and changing knee-jerk reactions and behavior. The whole point of studying human nature is to change it so it does not destroy the human race.

To do that, we must make the connection between what is in here and what is out there. We have to stop thinking we can do whatever we want, that our personal mental, physical, verbal bullets are not heard around the world. Bullets find their mark. And so does kindness.

What Can Happen to Teens because of Their Brains

Remembering that your brain is wired by what you are born with as well as what happens to you, you'll see that it's your reactions to your experiences, not just the experiences themselves, that make you what you are. Even more important is the intelligence you bring (not I.Q., but awareness, insight) to every situation, in the decisions about your own thoughts and behavior, and therefore your 'self'. *Because it is behavior that will make you what you are, not just what you were born with; not just what's been done to you—but what you do about all that.* You cannot change what you were born with or what's been done to you in the past. But you don't have to be a slave to your past—you can change what you do about it. This is how you rewire your brain. So we're after clarity, and the ability to learn and change, not just life choices made out of fear or confusion or habit—or someone else's authority.

Here are some of the scenarios teens can avoid, survive, or drown in:

- Drugs, alcohol, sex

- Early marriage, teen pregnancy

- Mental disorders like schizophrenia, depression, ADD, learning and developmental disorders

- Violence, jail, gangs, crime

- Competition, self-hate

- War: between nations (teenage soldiers are again dying in battle), between colors, classes, sexes

WHO AM I? WHAT AM I? AM I?

These are some of the types of personalities, the kinds of brains teens notice among themselves:

- Jock brain; physical competition

- Science and math brain; mental competition

- Writer's, actor's, musician's, and artist's brain; making and living in their own worlds

- Genius and techie brains; the need to understand how everything works

- Addict's brain; escapists, romance and sex junkies, violence and crime junkies, drug and alcohol addicts

- Popular brain; cool kids, the in-hip-hot crowd, approval-seekers, politicians

- The wild brains, the dreamers; new world revolutionists, mystics, rebels

- Mental illness, personality disorders, social misfits— impaired brains

The Teen Brain Book can help you to find out who and what you are now, then to make your own map, and learn to wire and keep on rewiring your own brain circuitry whenever you need to change yourself.

CHAPTER TWO

What Do I Do with My Life?
How Do I Find Out?—Who's Got the Map?—What's My Story?

Remembering that the physical brain's best-kept secret is how it creates your self, it's up to you to explore your brain and discover its maps and programs, its genetic, cultural, family conditioning, and the personal experiences you have added on to our human history. You have to do this, so your brain can't take you by surprise and push you this way when you want to go that way. In other words, you have to read and keep daily track of your own story in your own brain, or treat yourself as your own psychological case history, however you like to put it.

As we have discovered, your brain has both those capabilities: it can think up a self—and it can also look at that self and change it. This happens when you have an insight into the ways your self is hurting you, and rewiring your patterns by changing your attitudes and behavior.

For your own sake you must have the freedom to change your brain. For everyone's sake, we must all change. The philosopher J. Krishnamurti and theoretical physicist David Bohm held many dialogues (see *The Ending of Time: J. Krishnamurti & D. Bohm*) about the way of changing the human brain. For millions of years, our brains have been set in a pattern of self-family-tribe-nation-protective aggression and fear. Government laws, even great religious leaders, have tried to change us. If any external law, any wise teaching, was going to work, it would have worked by now. The fact is, it's an inside job!

Each of us must do it for ourselves. Each of us must change her or his own brain, stop the fear and the angry pain it causes. And we each have the tool: the mind. Call it mind, insight, intelligence, the capacity to see ourselves as we are and what our brains are doing to us because of all those messages from the past, collective and personal. Organizations and governments can't change us; we've tried all kinds of governments and all kinds of religions. Science can't change us; for all our technological advances, we are still savages in designer clothes. Not even drugs alone can change us. Drugs, pharmacological discoveries, only work a temporary or superficial change. We know because many of us have tried all that. More and more education and training of the intellect doesn't work, either. As Krishnamurti said, "Training the intellect does not result in intelligence...Until you really approach all of life with your intelligence, instead of merely your intellect, no system in the world will save man...."

A teen brain is exciting, flexible, because, as neuropsychiatrist Richard Restak puts it in his book *The Secret Life of the Brain*, "the child...is locked into the here and now, the adolescent can think in terms of imagined possibilities... brood about complex problems." Teen brains, more complex than a child's brain, more flexible than adult brains, can easily move back and forth between brain and mind, intellectual thought and insight.

Since the point of all this is the ability of a teenager to rewire his or her own brain, to lay new tracks, new nerve or neuronal circuits, some neuroscience, brain science, might be interesting.

Some Brain Science

Our brains adapt to the environment. Environment acts on genes as long as we live. Neuroscience, the study of the brain and the physiological links between the brain and the mind and behavior, tells us that our selves, our personalities, change, adapt, and adjust because our brain circuits continually wire and rewire to cope with our lives.

The brain is a large, soft mass of nerve tissue contained within the cranium portion of the skull. It is composed of

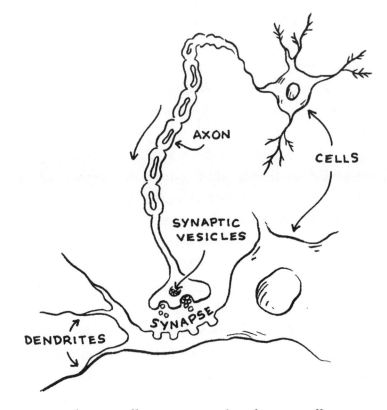

neurons (nerve cells, gray matter) and nerve cell processes (white matter, tracts connecting various parts of the brain with each other). What we call wiring is the path of connections between the brain's nerve cells. Brain cells are not fused directly to each other. They are connected instead by constant electrical and chemical activity that carries messages between the cells. A stimulated nerve cell fires a tiny electrical signal along a cell's axon until it arrives at the tiny space between cells called a synapse. Then electrical information is passed on, across the space, through chemistry. A messenger chemical, called a neurotransmitter, is released from the sending cell, across the space/synapse, to receptors of the receiving cell, which in turn send an electrical signal along the dendrite.

That is the basic information highway. More will be described in later chapters (for the main areas of the physical brain, see Chapter Four), but we need to understand from the beginning that thought, information processing, is physical. The brain is physical, what it does is physical, its thought processes are physical. A good intellect is not the result of the raw number of neurons in the brain; it has to do with the number of interconnections. A healthy personality or self is not the result of more brain cells or less brain cells, but which paths between cells are used when.

Modern technology can show us just how physical our thoughts are. Neuroscientists have PET scans (positron emission tomography) and MRI scans (magnetic resonance imaging) to watch the entire brain in action as it thinks, feels, and directs our actions and behaviors. Scans can even trace the effects of specific genes and neurotransmitters. And they keep finding new types of brain cells, or neurons, and neurotransmitters, the chemicals by which nerve cells communicate with each other. But as science writer John Horgan puts it in his book *The Undiscovered Mind*, "The Humpty-Dumpty dilemma…plagues not only neuroscience but also evolutionary psychology, cognitive science, artificial intelligence—scientists can take the brain apart, but have no idea how to put it back together again."

Yet while scientists still face some mysteries, they do understand a great deal about human nature, about the formation of the self in our brains. The story of the self forms in our brains out of the words it finds there, creating me. As philosopher and neuroscientist Daniel Dennett says in *Consciousness Explained*, "The strangest and most wonderful constructions in the whole animal world are the amazing, intricate constructions made by the primate, *Homo sapiens*. Each normal individual of this species makes a *self*. Out of its brain it spins a web of words and deeds, and, like the other creatures, it doesn't have to know what it's doing; it just does it....Our fundamental tactic of self-protection...is... controlling the story we tell others—and ourselves—about who we are." About dissociative identity disorder, in which a single human body seems to be shared by several selves, Dennett says that "two or three or seventeen selves per body is really no more metaphysically extravagant than one self per body!" More selves is just more stories.

Only still we ask what, exactly, is a self? What is this self, too often frightened and angry, sometimes lonely and insecure, moody, conflicted, alternately dazzled with joy and drowning in despair, spinning with sexuality, frustrated by authority, panting for freedom and yet terrified by the burden of paying its own rent? And, since the brain automatically creates a self or selves, and this self or these selves go on adding on to themselves, what is the way of observing this so this recorded self can't hurt us or others?

WHAT DO I DO WITH MY LIFE?

Self Is Thought

What we come back to over and over again is that it is thought based on memory that creates a self. Without thought and its words, there is no self. Most of us have not been educated about the origin of the self, the personality. Or else we have been given vague suggestions about essences, spirits, reincarnations, immortal souls.

Language, that basic human survival tool, is partly to blame for the confusion over the reality of the self: our language teaches us to say 'I' over and over again. "I feel." "I think." "I see." Instead of, more accurately, "This organism, this brain and body, feels, thinks, sees." Cultural inoculations like giving us personal names, parent-love, religion, schooling, perpetuates what language encourages, the separate "I."

But in Dennett's words, actually, when you look for an occupant, *"there's nobody home"*—except what your brain's thoughts based on culture and language invent.

But don't take other people's word about the origin of your self. Try an experiment of your own. Try stopping yourself from thinking. You can play ball, dance, stare at a tree or a candle. If you stop thought, you'll find there isn't any self. The 'you' of you disappears, and there is just attention in your brain. Notice the next time you have been so occupied with something you like to do, you suddenly jolt back to the present with words like, "I have got to get back to my life (my homework, the dishes, my next class)." If you are deeply paying attention to something, a sport, someone you love, a movie—you disappear for a while. Then thought cranks up again, says something like "pull yourself together," and there you are, chattering away to yourself inside your own head in a chorus of different voices. You can prove to yourself that your self is really your own soap opera, the ongoing story you tell yourself about your life.

You can change the story any time you like. You can change the story of yourself by making a decision to think differently, or behave differently, or adopt a new attitude. This isn't a matter of someone else's authority; no one else, no teacher or therapist, can do this for you. A good teacher can point out the general problems of the brain, but you have to brainwash yourself—that is, literally, physically, change your own brain's nerve cells' circuits. Change any piece of your behavior or environment, change any attitude, for a period of time, and you change the brain's pathways. A good example of this is among teen addicts in recovery. Others can relate their own experiences, counseling and meetings can give support and information, but teens have to learn for themselves that the attitude change and action is up to them. *The past doesn't change; but they can change the present every new moment and therefore the future.* If they don't pick up, they don't get high; if they don't want to pick up, they don't go where the drugs are. And no one except themselves can do this for them. This change in attitude, behavior and environment actually, physically, changes the brain. This ability to change is especially possible in the natural development of the teen years when the brain wants to mature anyway so it can be more independent of its parents. Don't let anyone tell you teenagers are just unaccountably changeable, moody, and rebellious. The teen brain is simply growing new connections, "as a tree growing extra roots, branches, and twigs," as Restak describes it. The teen brain is pruning its own brain cells, forming and reforming its own pathways, so it can plan its own life instead of depending on its parents' frontal lobes to tell it to eat, work, and come in out of the rain.

Use it or lose it. Wire by firing, as neuroscientist Joseph LeDoux says. Remember, the brain's pathways—its wiring— are simply the chemical/electrical connections between nerve cells. These synapses, these pathways, are the main channels of information flow and storage in the brain. As LeDoux points out in his book *Synaptic Self: How Our Brains Become Who We Are*, "the brain makes the self" through its synapses: the brain's synaptic connections provide the biological base for memory, which makes possible the sense of continuity and permanence fundamental to the conception of the self.

The basic facts are simple.

Your self, or your personality, is physical. It is wired by repetitive use in your brain. Some neural systems, some memory, some learning in humans has existed throughout the evolutionary history of mammals, vertebrates, life itself. Some memory and learning systems are wired by family history, personal experience. The repetitive use of certain pathways, whether of behavior or self-talk, deepens and strengthens the track. For example, I play the piano, football, my girlfriend's or boyfriend's name is Gloria or Sam, my father is a baker named George, I get good/bad marks, I feel great/dorky, I am I—all this repetitive use of the same pathways over and over makes them very powerful and hard to override. Changing yourself actually involves simply not using those same old pathways. Non-use weakens the connections of words and behaviors and eventually fades them out. A good for-instance is: you don't have to tell yourself you are terrific to make yourself feel good (which you may not believe anyway). Just stop your brain from calling yourself a jerk. You'll automatically feel better.

Actually, neuroscientists are discovering what metaphysical philosophers have always known. Simply this: you can change the wiring, fade the old out, fade in the new.

Simple, of course, does not mean easy. Changing yourself is hard to do.

It's one thing to understand what we have been talking about: philosophy, developmental psychology, evolution, cognitive science, neuroscience. We can understand the hardware of humanity, its brain, and the software programs historically and personally. But all this, while interesting, isn't much use in stopping the pain a teenager feels or inflicts, unless we all, teen and adult, change our own wiring and create a mutation every day in our own brains. Just as you cannot hold onto joy, love, and companionship forever, you cannot make anger or fear or loneliness go away forever.

You can only deal with them properly each time they appear. States of being pass anyway: you can just let them go.

So the answer to "what do I do with my life" and "who's got the map" — is you!

CHAPTER THREE

What's Your Story?
The Wiring and Rewiring of Three Teens

"To suffer psychologically is to live in pain and isolation. It is a lonely place to live, especially when you think no one else is like you, or even understands," says Hannah Carlson, author and past director of Developmental Disabilities for the Kennedy Center. Whether temporary or long-term, serious or moderate, psychological illness and suffering is the loss of the ability to function appropriately in everyday life. It's very lonely. What people want when they suffer such sadness is understanding. Do you, or does any-one you know, identify with the following stories? Use these three teens as a mirror in which to see yourself, wholly or partly.

Dana: Depression in a Romance Junkie

Dana's Feelings

By the time Dana was fifteen, she knew that unless she was in love she wanted to die. Other girls were happy going to clubs, movies, or school games and dances in groups, if they weren't dating someone special. But not Dana.

"Dana's intense," said her best friend Claudia. "If she's not desperately in love, she's miserable, like she's living under a black cloud or something."

Dana knew this was true. Dating was not a game with her, as it was with other girls, or a way to be popular, or just a feather in her cap. It wasn't even interesting to her to date a lot of different boys, as her mother hoped she would. She found it superficial and boring to be with someone who wasn't really meaningful to her, who didn't make her feel as if she were flying without wings. What Dana wanted in a boyfriend was someone who made her insides melt, her heart speed, her brain flame, who set her whole life on fire. What this required was a boy like Mike, who was as lonely and as desperate as Dana was herself, who needed her as much as she needed him. When they were together, they were high, blazing. When they were apart, they suffered the withdrawal symptoms of a drug down, deep depression as if they had fallen into a black hole.

Dana's Problem

Sometimes mental disorders can interfere with the proper development of the brain's nerve circuits. In the crowded complexity of the network of connections that wire a maturing brain, it's hardly surprising that mistakes happen in the pattern of transmission, that wires get crossed or neurons send and receive the wrong or insufficient chemical messages (neurotransmitters like dopamine, serotonin, norepinephrine, acetylcholine). Science is not totally certain about the chemical details of depression, except that it is a brain disease that results from a chemical imbalance in the parts of the brain important in generating emotion, especially in the limbic system of the brain, including the amygdala. In adolescence the emotion system is still maturationally ahead of the judgement system anyway: depression only makes the problem worse.

Mental illness, like other personality characteristics, is a product of both genes and environment. Parental genes for chemical imbalance and her home environment affect Dana. Both Dana's parents, particularly her mother, suffered from depression. Both drank too much, and when they drank, they fought, blaming their depressions on each other. One of her parents' ways of climbing out of their own depressions was to rely on Dana to entertain them, to make them feel good about themselves as parents, to pick up their spirits, by living up to their standards for her. This included lots of boyfriends, eventually the 'right' boyfriend, and a good marriage after good college and career choices. It was the usual parental dream: only Dana's parents were missing the truth about Dana. She was bright, capable, and at some level agreed with her parents about her life. But she was also unable to help herself from disappointing them all. According to Hannah Carlson in her book *The Courage to Lead: Start Your Own Support Group—Mental Illnesses and Addictions*, Dana was among the more than 19 million people in the United States affected by major depression, now the most common disability in America, with more than 35,000 suicides per year, especially among women between the ages of fifteen and thirty. And Dana, like her parents, remained undiagnosed and untreated, though treatment is possible now through therapy and/or with the new antidepressant drugs available such as Prozac, Zoloft, and Paxil.

Assessment

Like many depressed people, Dana and her parents were self-medicating. PET scans show that frontal lobe activity (thinking things through) in depressed people is not properly balancing the emotional centers (feeling too much). So what Dana and her parents did to balance themselves was to tone down, deaden, all the emotions of fear, anxiety, guilt, worthlessness, dread, restless irritability, all the emptiness and suicidal pessimism and rage that are the symptoms of depression.

Her parents anaesthetized those feelings with alcohol, or else blamed their bad feelings on each other and Dana.

Dana blamed her bad feelings on her parents, and anaesthetized them with the high of being in love. *The brain chemistry of being in love is just as visible in the MRI scans of brain structures as drug use.* Subjects are shown pictures of friends, then pictures of someone who really turns them on. Not only are specific structures in the middle of the brain activated, but the amygdala and other brain regions responsible for depression and anxiety are deactivated. Falling in love is one way of escaping problems instead of learning to solve them; using this technique over and over establishes and maintains immature brain patterns that can last into a lifetime of 'love affairs,' marriages, and divorces.

Rewiring

Imagine what some education in neuroscience, some psychotherapy, not to console but to learn the ways of the human psyche, appropriate drug treatment, and above all understanding and clarity could do for this family. For now, however, Dana's parents continue to brood, fight with each other in their own misery and over Dana's life, and blame her miseries on each other. What Dana is learning is a pattern of blaming instead of responsibility in repairing her own hurt. What Dana is learning most from them is that in between her highs from romance, alcohol can do the same thing: provide a respite, a temporary high by deadening the bad feelings. Dana is the result of genetic predisposition toward chronic, clinical depression and addiction. She is also the result of the environment in her parents' home of suffering and escape, rather than suffering and learning from it in order to rewire and change it.

Dana, unless she changes, will grow up not only dangerous to herself but to other people. Damaged people are dangerous; they know they can survive their own messes, and so continue to make messes. None of this suffering and possessive dependency is love, no matter what people call it. The measure of love is not pain: it is an affectionate state of being, attitudes, and behavior toward all life. What Dana calls being in love is really only person addiction. And with addiction comes need, not love.

Mike: Violence and Crime

Mike's Feelings
At sixteen, Mike could not remember a time when he wasn't angry. If he looked back for the sweetness of any childhood memory, a Christmas toy, a walk on a summer beach, his rage corrupted the past moment as it corrupted the present. Mike was good at anger. He had been taught by experts. There were times he amused himself by trying to decide if he was more furious at his father for beating him and his mother, or at his mother who knew exactly the words and gestures to torment and provoke his father—and then submitted passively to the abuse.

The first sweet moments of his life were when Dana fell in love with him and he with her. It was instant chemistry. They were rehearsing Shakespeare's *A Midsummer Night's Dream* on the school's outdoor stage on a spring evening. When he bent his head over hers to speak a line, she raised her eyes to his. Something electric happened. He could feel the blaze from his brain travel down his spine to between his legs and up again. Mike realized two things instantly: this was the girl he wanted to marry; and he had to make absolutely certain she never found out about his other life.

In school, except for a few incidents over the years when he got into serious trouble for fighting and injuring classmates, putting his fist through a sheetrock wall, once nearly destroying an empty classroom, Mike kept a fairly low profile. With his tall, dark good looks, his fists, and his ability with racing fast cars, he commanded a certain respect from his classmates, but they sensed something was wrong with Mike, and Mike knew there was something wrong with him. He had a couple of buddies. Hugo was a science genius, beyond anything high school could teach him. Jack was a computer genius who also built bombs in his garage lab; he had dyslexia and no interest whatsoever in anything high school could teach him.

The three friends spent the secret part of their lives in Hugo's basement—his parents traveled—getting high, dealing drugs, and leaving in the dark middle of the night only long enough to rob deli's and gas stations and occasionally the apartments of absent friends' parents, for money and electronic equipment to fence for drugs.

Mike's Problem

According to Steve Hyman, the director of the National Institute of Mental Health, "An adolescent at risk for addiction starts off with something like attention deficit disorder, depression...a difficult temperament...the healthy, well-socialized peer group doesn't like them; their teachers don't like them; even their parents can barely tolerate them." Miserable at school and at home, isolated outsiders who feel separate, different, rejected by everybody else, they are misfits and loners who seek each other for support in commiseration and in finding ways to stop their sense of painful isolation and rage.

Mike's pain is his anger based on a lifelong terror of his father, and a growing terror that if he sees his father raise a hand to his mother one more time, he'll kill the old man. Awake, Mike is too big for his father to beat up any more. But the boy in him still sweats in his dreams. And he takes his rage out on everything and everyone around him, and in destroying his own life.

Assessment

The brain has pleasure centers. These get fired up naturally by food, by sex, by exercise, by music and warmth and beauty, and with such stimulation the chemical messengers, the pleasure neurotransmitters, especially dopamine, ripple along the brain's circuits.

Addictive drugs mimic natural neurotransmitters with an electrochemical surge greater than winning a race, a lover, an award, sometimes even greater than orgasm. They invade pleasure circuits, until healthy pleasures, unused, have no effect. In its drugged, isolated state, the teen brain fails to develop a healthy prefrontal cortex with its judgement and its moral responsibility; therefore, understanding the consequences of drug-taking, the violent, even criminal behavior of securing drugs and drug money is stunted. The personality is transformed. The trouble, of course, with addictive drugs, is that taking them sets you up for needing more. As Shakespeare said, "appetite grows by what it feeds on." And some drugs, Ecstasy, for instance, can do even more than invade and addict and retard development. Ecstasy is a drug that is actually neurotoxic. It has LSD effects. It destroys nerve cells. It affects areas of the brain responsible for learning and memory.

Rewiring
From pot to cocaine, from angel dust to Ecstasy to heroin to alcohol, to nicotine, which is, after all, just another drug, all addictive, mood-altering drugs behave like terrorists hijacking the brain-reward neural pathways, giving your brain instant false, temporary rewards and what is worse, setting your brain up to need the next jolt. The healthy reward circuits, unused, are beginning to disappear.

Rewiring an addict's brain is the hardest rewiring job there is because, in drug use, pleasure and relief from anxiety are so instant. You don't have to work for it, or even wait for relief. It's like a baby with a bottle; gratification is immediate. The trouble is, that unlike a baby with milk, what the addict takes into the system is poison that destroys the brain.

Rewiring the brain means changing its patterns. Change begins with the easiest part: hands off, don't pick up. The hardest part follows: change every attitude, behavior, person, place, or thing in the addict's life associated with drugging and drinking, so that one day at a time, new habits of thinking and behavior are formed. Then new neural pathways, circuits, are formed so an addict's brain no longer sends uncontrollable signals to pick up again. As neuroscientist Joseph LeDoux says in *Synaptic Self*, "The essence of who we are is encoded in our brains, and brain changes account for the alterations of thought, mood, and behavior....Mental states...are accounted for by intricate patterns of information processing within and between synaptically connected neural circuits."

Change the information you input into your brain, and you change your brain's circuits and your brain's output.

Claudia: Early Marriage, Teen Pregnancy, and Anxiety Disorder

Claudia's Feelings
By the time Claudia was seventeen she had two babies. She had been married, divorced, and was now married again to the father of the second baby. She had just discovered she was pregnant again. To her parents and among her friends, Claudia, knowing what was expected of her from past experience, said all the right things. "Not again. I don't believe

it! But we used protection. How could this happen to me? I really wanted to finish high school this time."

Secretly, Claudia was exhilarated. But she could only admit this to her friend Dana. They were in the same class even though Claudia was older, because Claudia kept taking time out from school to have babies.

"What does Chuck think?" Dana asked Claudia. Chuck, once their high school's football team hero and now its coach, was Claudia's husband.

"A man who doesn't want babies I don't want," Claudia said.

There had never been a time Claudia had not felt anxious, nervous, worried, absolutely phobic, she often told Dana, about how less-than-everybody-else she felt. She was always afraid socially, wherever she went in school, at home, in a store buying clothes, at a beach party with her friends, that she was being criticized: that she was stupid, or fat, or her hair was wrong. She didn't belong, she wasn't like other people. For days on end, Claudia hid in her room, refused to leave the house. Her parents were at a loss about what to do for their daughter. They had adopted Claudia because they were not able to have a child of their own, and they adored her. Because they loved her, they couldn't understand why Claudia did not love herself—unless she was pregnant. Unless she was creating little beings who looked like her, who needed her, who belonged to her. If she could people her own world with her own flesh and blood, she need never feel like an outsider again.

Claudia's Problem

Claudia has an anxiety disorder. Anxiety is distinct from fear which is a perceived physical threat such as a Tiger Woods golf ball aimed at your head. Anxiety is not the fear of something that is happening to you; it is the worry over something that might happen to you. There are many kinds of anxiety disorders: free-floating anxiety; specific phobias or fears of something in particular; panic disorders; post-traumatic stress disorders; and obsessive-compulsive disorders, to name a few.

Claudia's anxiety disorder is a social phobia, the psychological fear of other people's negative opinion of her and *its imagined power to hurt her*. All people worry about this from time to time, just as all people have down moods from time to time. But just as Dana's clinical depression is a chronic state that keeps her stuck in a dark hole for long periods of time, and just as Mike's drugged violence worsens his own and other's lives, Claudia's anxiety disorders her life and will affect her husband, and the futures of possibly too many babies.

Anxiety disorder is a mental state in which, says LeDoux, "the systems involved in emotional processing, such as the amygdala, have detected a threatening situation, and are influencing...working memory." Again, fear is a reaction to an actual threat: anxiety is worrying over what might happen. Pathological (diseased) behavior, as a result of anxiety disorder, is an exaggerated avoidance of imagined threats, repeated over and over again, using the same neural paths over and over again.

Assessment

To avoid worrying about the imagined harm of other people's imagined negative opinions about her, Claudia was trying to populate a private world where she could be forever safe.

Claudia knew her parents loved her, perhaps even more because she was so wanted that she was adopted. But knowing something and feeling it can be different experiences in different circuits of the brain. The business of knowing something, as we will discover in later chapters, involves the prefrontal cortex and the workings of learning, memory, experience. Claudia's anxiety, however, involves the feeling parts of her brain, the limbic system, the amygdala. In her teens, Claudia is immature in judgement, overwhelmed by her emotional systems, and both uneducated and inexperienced in handling her feelings. Moreover, the feelings she has about not sharing a known gene pool—after all, no one could say truthfully to her that she has her father's eyes or her mother's smile or her grandmother's bossiness—have made her determined to create a gene pool of her own.

Rewiring

Because Claudia's original parents are unknown, there is no easy way to discover whether the original genetic pool included a predisposition toward anxiety disorder. Not that it will matter to Claudia any more than the genetic origin of our disorders should matter to any but biological psychiatrists. Our problems, whether dumped on us or not, are still ours, and they are our responsibility to solve.

In Claudia's case, what will be useful is education about how the brain works, especially the developmental stages of a teenager's brain, and the reassurance that her judgement faculty will catch up to her emotional life so her feelings won't override her brain all the time. What will be further necessary is cognitive therapy, so she can talk to a therapist about her feelings, understand them so she can change the ways she feels, thinks, and believes, which is the process of talk therapy. She will also need some behavioral therapy with its emphasis on changing her behavior, the ways she acts. CBT—cognitive and behavioral therapy—is often supported, for anxiety disorders as for depression and schizophrenia, by the use of medication.

What is exciting in all this is that, as LeDoux says, "experience is often considered the counterpoint to genes." New understanding, new behavior, new experiences both because of ordinary maturation—just growing older—and through insight into how the brain works, all this is stored as synaptic changes in the brain.

The human brain can transform itself. It's the most extraordinary, the best news there is. The only hard part is we have to do the work ourselves. Other people can encourage, cheer us on, share their information, their own experience, even their strength. But information and other people's experience is like reading about air; if you don't breathe it yourself, it doesn't do you much good.

What's Your Story?

With the pattern, the method, of the discussion of the histories of Dana, Mike, and Claudia, you can begin to describe your own life, your own mental state, the ways, healthy and otherwise, you solve your own problems. What is important here is not someone else's evaluation, but how you feel in your own skin, and especially in your own brain.

The outline Hannah Carlson suggests is a S.O.A.P.

- SUBJECTIVE: the problem seen from your own perspective

- OBJECTIVE: the problem seen from someone else's perspective (you might ask a good friend, a close but fair friend, to describe you and your life and problems)

- ASSESSMENT: diagnosis, meaning what is wrong, if there is anything wrong—do some reading (psychology, neuroscience, philosophy, physics, and metaphysics), ask peers who have experiences like yours, check with a school therapist or counselor

- PRESCRIPTION: what to do about what is wrong; what is necessary in order to change what is wrong, in your thinking, your ideas, your feelings, above all your attitudes and behavior, so your brain can transform itself. It must transform itself so it can deal with pain when life hands it out. After all, as Krishnamurti said, "if you are hurt, you have a problem." The hurt is in you, and only you can deal with it.

CHAPTER FOUR

Am I Really Free?

Or Am I Just a Program, and, if so, Hard-Wired or Software?—How Learning and Memory Work

The Brain Records Everything

'You' are your brain's connections—'you' are not some mini-me in there, not some ghost haunting your own brain. But how did 'you' get wired into circuits, how did 'you' get downloaded in the first place?

Whatever your story about yourself and your problems, whatever Dana's depression and person-dependency addiction, whatever Mike's rage and drug addiction, whatever Claudia's obsessive pregnancies—all of this is recorded in the brain. It is observable by neuroscientists in PET scans and MRIs of the brain's activities. A whole new world of self-understanding—what philosophers, anthropologists, sociologists, psychologists, the great religious teachers have been saying for centuries is the key to happiness and joy in living—is now technologically available. The new neuroscience may eventually lead to our understanding as well about how the brain actually works, since while we understand the brain in its parts, we do not yet understand how the whole works together. Since the brain is responsible not only for our own personalities, but for our whole world culture, for reason and memory, for language and behavior, it is amazing to people who think about such things that we haven't devoted more time to understanding the human brain. We seem to spend more time tinkering with cars and computers than with our brains. And we know more about cyberspace than inner space.

Computers/Brain Science

Part of the problem is, according to Harvard Medical School psychiatrist John Ratey, that too much of mind/brain science is described in computer language. In *A User's Guide to the Brain*, Ratey says, "The brain is nothing like the personal computers it has designed, for it does not process information and construct images by manipulating strings of digits such as ones and zeros....Most...functions involve the interaction...from many different parts of the brain at once; it is the bane of cognitive scientists that bananas are not located in a single structure of the brain." Ratey's view of the functions of the human brain is not a mechanical one; it is like that of ecosystems. Memory, for instance, is not stored in one place. Thoughts and feelings are not assembled from locatable bits of data. Thoughts and feelings, healthy perceptions or mental deficits are the result of interactions of different suborgans and subsystems and subcircuits all over the brain. The search for a single gene or a single neuron is not going to help cure what it takes a whole group of systems to perceive.

So, every part of the brain can affect other parts. The trouble with one system can affect or infect others. A biological developmental deficit, a simple problem with one physical perception such as hearing properly can cause other parts of the brain to stop functioning properly, so that thinking is affected, feelings are affected, and social impairments, such as loss of self-respect and a sense of failure, are recorded in the brain's circuits as well.

An artist I know, while she is visually brilliant, has a brain with a problem in processing what she hears. When she was in school, she was diagnosed with everything from mild retardation to ADD to oppositional defiant disorder. The artist's self-observation later on helped her therapist to determine that the malfunctioning system was just her hearing, that she was neither stupid nor a failure. Shame, guilt, self-hate lifted with the understanding of the organic problem. And some hard psychological work on the artist's part retrained her brain to perceive herself differently, to rewire her behavioral circuits. She is now able to be married, to be a mother, and to be a successful artist and teacher, none of which had once been possible. Testing, diagnosis, and treatment are all available now. These can help teens especially not to misperceive themselves or start their adult lives feeling worthless or inadequate.

Sometimes we are stuck with faulty genes. Sometimes we're stuck with parents too self-absorbed with their own problems to pick up on our childhood troubles. We land in our teens with a genetic and environmental mess in our psyches. *But what happens from then on is our own responsibility.* Blaming, judging, and condemning yourself or others, is a silly waste of time and energy. Just observation, which is a moment-to-moment business, just learning all the time, not accumulating but ongoing looking at yourself and everything around you, will save your brain. As Krishnamurti says, "There is no end to learning; learning is all important, not the failures, successes, and mistakes."

Are We Hard-Wired?

The brain, it turns out, is so complex, so dynamic, so plastic and changeable, that we can stop being afraid we're too hardwired to change. That human nature is too genetically hard-wired to change itself can be disproved by the fact that it is virtually impossible to predict how a brain will respond to its genes. Sibling studies, even twins studies, of alcoholics cannot account for 1) why one will become an alcoholic and the other not, or even 2) why one will succeed in a recovery program and the other not. As Ratey says, "Scientists can no more predict how a given brain will express a gene than predict what a tropical jungle will look like in thirty years....In a system as complex as our brain, it really is up to us, and this is why it is so crucial that we learn about our brains. We do have free will...everything we do affects everything that follows...changing your habits and lifestyle to live the most productive life you can."

The image of a jungle is not a bad one for the brain, which looks like an overgrown jungle of 100 billion nerve cells, or neurons. Each nerve cell has one axon and up to 100,000 dendrites. Dendrites are the main way neurons get information, that is, LEARN. Axons are the main way neurons pass on information, that is, TEACH other neurons.

The pathways are not predetermined and fixed: they can alter throughout our lives, either strengthening like muscles through active use and practice, or withering away like the atrophied muscles of a couch potato.

The Wiring of Learning and Memory: How Does It Happen?

Evolutionary neuroscientist Steven Pinker's book *How the Mind Works* is a gene's eye view of the mind/brain. He says, "The mind is a system of organs of computation designed by natural selection." Pinker calls humans the nerds of the Earth in that we are the brainy animal that fills the cognitive niche. Our mental machinery invents technical machinery and so dominates the stronger, the swifter, the flighted, and all the other more athletic creatures. Humans approach, and other species drop like flies. *This is not a sign of greater intelligence. There is no such thing as general animal intelligence.* To Pinker, the neural network of the brain in every animal is an information processing machine that evolved to solve its problems, and we simply invent technology and machinery—both helpful and dangerous—to solve ours. Bacteria solve their problems with large numbers: if numbers were the criteria for importance, we would be living in the Age of Bacteria, not humans. That humans are here at all is not a sign of our superiority but a meteorological accident from the universe. If a meteor from outer space had not knocked out the dinosaurs, we would still be a tiny furry creature up a tree. As Gould says, we are only a twig somewhere on the bush of life. Only in our insecurity about our place in the universe, a kind of hopeful arrogance, and a passion for making up stories to tell our children, we invent a hierarchical tree with us as the tin star on top.

Learning

Our species has the longest of prolonged childhoods. This gives us a long, long apprenticeship for learning knowledge and skills. Our species is capable of language, and language is our means of exchanging and passing on knowledge, between people, and down the generations. This business of language means our information can build on itself, not just repeat in each individual, but add on and move on.

Dennett states that some elements of information are wired genetically into the parts of the brain responsible for eating, eliminating, breathing, reproduction, thirst, movement. These are 'given' to us in the way we are wired at birth. Other information must be learned, inputted like software. Learning occurs, he suggests, through responses of neural networks of activity in the cerebral cortex to both internal and external stimulation. This cortex he describes as the huge convoluted mantle (about 80% of the human brain) that developed in the human skull and completely covers the older animal brain underneath.

Innate learning is what we are born with.

Cultural learning is the second medium of the information in our brains, so that each of us does not have to reinvent the wheel.

So, learning is the recording by bundles of neurons and their synapses all over the brain, both wired-in at birth and acquired ever after through the electrical activity in the brain in response to the stimulation of experience. It's a complex process that is simple to prove: stick a pin in yourself and see what happens, physically, then mentally, in your thoughts and your emotions.

Memory

Memory is the word we use for stored-up information. We have short-term or working memory, located in the frontal lobe to hold small bits of data, ideas, and motivations for a few seconds, and then short-term memory counts on long-term memory to encode and process. Long-term memory's information is not stored in one place constituting any sort of 'I' or 'ego' or 'self' but all over the brain. (We can't even find where a bicycle is in our brains, much less 'you.')

Again, it would be much more accurate to say, "This organism sees that tree," than to say "I see that tree." (Actually, at the level of physics, neither is correct, as our brains simply organize oceans of light waves and billions of atoms so the human eye can see anything at all.)

All your selves, the sum, the collection of which we call 'yourself' is just those memories stored in your neural networks.

Genes, both throughout mammal and primate history, as well as your own family's history, inform the networks in your cortex, your hippocampus, your limbic system, and other brain regions. So you have inherited a lot of already-stored memory that directs the way you walk, talk, behave, feel, think, and see the world around you.

Your own life experiences constantly add ongoing information to your memory networks for additional processing and storage.

The Physical Brain: Thought, Consciousness, Intellect, Intelligence

Something you may already have noticed about the head housing the brain we speak of is that it is connected to the body, by the neck, by bones, muscles, ligaments, by blood flow, by various hormones produced by various glands. The brain in your head is connected as well to your circulatory, nervous, and reproductive systems, by complex chemistry, and also, actually, attitude. Attitudes formed in the brain inside your head produce acid and alkaline in the body's systems and can affect health, life/death situations, relationships to others negatively or positively.

I mention this connection because the main job of this brain, as we have said, is to keep this body alive. The physical brain, connected to the spinal cord, is the main organ of the nervous system, the control center for your whole body's voluntary and involuntary activities.

The main areas of the brain are:

The **brainstem**—controls vital, involuntary body functions like breathing, digestion, reflexes. It connects the brain to the spinal cord.

The **limbic system**—coordinates emotions and connects to the cognitive, prefrontal cortex for thought and judgement; a complex system of physical brain areas, the limbic system primarily comprises the amygdala, hippocampus, thalamus, and insula, and perhaps even more areas of the physical brain than we yet know.

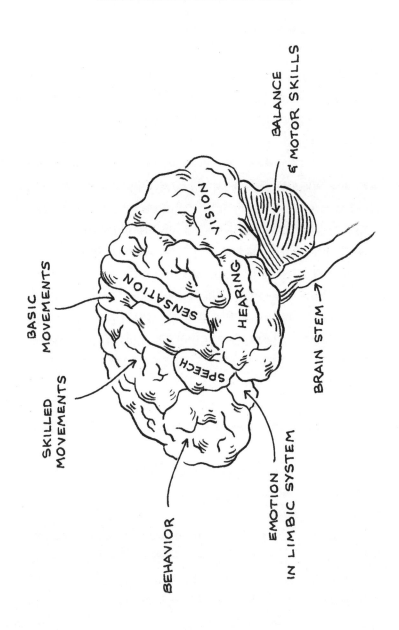

The **cerebellum**—coordinates body movements, balance, and holds us upright.

The **cerebrum**—the seat of consciousness, the center of our higher mental faculties such as learning, reasoning, judgement, intellect. It consists of right and left cerebral hemispheres; these are joined by the **corpus callosum**. Different areas of the cerebrum have different roles: speech; hearing; vision and visual recognition; basic and skilled movements; sensation; and, right in front, the **frontal cortex** which controls judgement, planning, problem-solving, short-term memory, behavioral decisions, and emotional sorting based on the limbic system's information.

The **cerebral cortex**—the wrinkled outer layer, full of gray matter, of the cerebral hemispheres of our brain. The **prefrontal cortex** performs executive functions of attention, working, short-term memory for data, motivations, ideas, higher-order cognition, decision-making. The systems that handle working memory count on the long-term memory system to encode the information in the hippocampus and other parts of the brain.

The Nervous System

The **nervous system** is made up of the brain, spinal cord, and nerves throughout the body. The nervous system is the body's electrochemical communication system, sending electrical impulses aided by chemical reactions from the brain throughout the body.

Information Input: from Outside, from Inside

The brain receives information basically in two ways: externally, through our five sense organs: eyes, ears, nose, tongue and palette, skin; and internally through memory—image formation—recognition, genetic, cultural conditioning. The biological, cultural, even gender and personal agenda, vary only superficially in our species. As the great poet Maya Angelou says, "We are more alike than unalike."

Teen girls take note: According to a 2001 *U.S. News & World Report* article, research suggests that the emotional brain is more primitive in men. Women make use of an emotional processing center near the speech areas of the brain, while men make use of an older reptilian system more closely linked with action.

The implications of this difference in the evolution of the brains of the sexes seem to be that the male brain is still closer to the brains of our hunter-fighter forebears. Understanding this will help males to be mindful of aggressive behavior. It will help females to understand why they are fearful in the face of that aggression, and to take action, and live full lives, not just express emotion.

Some Word Definitions, not Absolute, Just for Convenience

Thought: Thought is the brain's response to memory, to experience, which is the past. As Krishnamurti says, "You would have no thoughts if you had no memory, and the response of memory to a certain experience brings the thought processes into action." As Ratey puts it, "Thinking is indeed a process, a biological function performed by the brain...the act of receiving, perceiving, comprehending, storing, manipulating, monitoring, controlling, and responding to the steady stream of data." Thought also involves the *emotion* system; emotionally charged information, unless it is the primary flight-or-fight stimulus, is also modulated by thought.

Learning: Learning is the brain/body response to external and internal data in the present, observation, attention to what is, to what is actually happening right now.

Thought and knowledge are the past. Learning is always in the present, and necessary to understand anything new. Self is the past. Seeing is new.

Consciousness: Consciousness is all the contents of your memories, all your past inherited agendas, all your personal experiences and stories, all your selves, your self. Sigmund Freud, the father of Western psychoanalysis, taught that this content can be conscious (we can access it), unconscious (we have suppressed it), or subconscious (we have buried it deep). As we have pointed out, there is no single point in the brain where a self sits on a throne taking in information and handing out orders. We like to think this fairytale is true because it gives the brain a sense of security and continuity in this life and the hope of immortality in lives to come. Also, it feels as if you have a central self because thought has invented one, so it is hard to change your attitude about this. But the truth can change an attitude. *How you feel,* as the philosopher Ray Fisher says, *is not what you actually are.*

Consciousness, in fact, is more like an editorial process that takes place in many parts of the brain, continually revising its information into many versions, many drafts of observable reality. A great number of processes accomplish the editorial work of the brain, Dennett points out. *Memory, conditioning, experience, often stop the rewriting process to match a stored image in the brain, and new discovery, new learning, is halted.* Great scientists, religious philosophers like Jesus Christ, Lao Tzu, the Buddha, Krishnamurti, may draw on technological knowledge, but psychologically they stay awake: they keep on learning and discovering, constantly tuning their behavior and insight to whatever is happening in the moment, not living according to past rules and yesterday's information.

Consciousness is still an enormous mystery to scientists. "Consciousness presents us with puzzle after puzzle, " says neuroscientist and psychologist Steven Pinker. "How can a neural event cause consciousness to happen?" And writer and biologist Thomas Huxley wondered how it is that "anything so remarkable as a state of consciousness comes about as a result of irritating nervous tissue."

Despite some differences in the actual definition of the word consciousness, what everyone seems to agree on is that consciousness has something to do with being self-aware and aware that we are aware of ourselves and other phenomena, the stuff of existence—in other words, smart. Lest, however, we puff ourselves up about being smart, remember that being smart is only one survival adaptation in the history of evolution. Keep in mind longevity—we have only lived a fraction of the time dinosaurs, who lived for 165 million years, ruled the Earth—and numbers. Think of the bacteria!

Simply, then, consciousness is the contents of your thoughts, feelings, fears, pleasures, worries about sex, failure, your dreams, your happinesses—all of that which is you.

Intellect and Intelligence

Intellect is knowledge, information.

Intelligence is insight into what to do with the above.

When Krishnamurti founded schools in California, England, and India, he insisted that the whole young person be educated, that information and intellect be put in the context of intelligent use of it, that an obsession with information overload can destroy the quality of a mind that simply can't turn off thought and has no relationship with nature, family, other people, and the rest of the world, even its own body and sensory responses. He was concerned that young people lost in the addictive computer and television screen, in information accumulation, have abandoned the ability to discover anything new for themselves. They have grown addicted to authority, dependent as robots or cultists, on somebody else to answer all their questions.

Today's teenagers think faster than any previous generation. As technology speeds up delivery of information, thinking speeds up. As schools increase the volume of tests about information, and the teaching of how to take tests and sort information, the information overload especially for higher education exams becomes more crazy-making than useful. This is because the mere collection of information bears little relationship to intelligence or intelligent living. It is all in the sorting out, in the proper application, and this includes information about the body, the brain, the self and its ways, the interrelationship of all life and activity on the planet and the universe.

The Life of Your Brain

The developmental stages of your brain—fetus; child; teenager; mature adult; old age—will be tracked in the second section of this book, as will the details of activity in some of your brain's more interesting areas.

For now, I think Ratey's description of the human brain as having what he calls Four Theaters is useful. He describes the brain's major functions—movement, memory, language, emotion, and social ability—this way:

1. Theater One: Perception—captures incoming stimuli.

2. Theater Two: Attention and Conscious Cognition—filter these perceptions.

3. Theater Three: Brain Functions—these work on the information, creating movement, memory, emotion, language, images.

4. Theater Four: The result of all the above is behavior, social ability, identity—in short, the self, with all its particular ways of talking, walking, thought patterns, problems, emotional states, and personality quirks.

What you say affects—even infects—what you think, not the other way around. That in mind, we really need to understand and think truthfully, even if we don't say it out loud, 'this organism sees,' not 'I see' and 'this brain records,' not 'I remember,' so language does not constantly corrupt your brain. If you lose the habit of repeating 'I' all the time to yourself, you may indeed lose the habit of self and all its fears. The brain is not a prisoner, after all, either of its genes or what has been stuffed into it. It can rewire itself. It can create a whole new way of living life.

CHAPTER FIVE

Am I Unique, Or Like Everyone Else?
More Teen Stories

Yes. To both questions. The distance at which moms can pick out their own kids on a soccer field is pretty small as universal distances go. From a helicopter, it's just scrambled boys and girls. Up closer, a mom can separate out her own two: Ben, the kinesthetic genius (jock and class hero), and Jack, science and computer techie (Mike's friend and favorite nerd). Like snowflakes, we are all different. Like snowflakes, we are all alike. As high school teacher Anna

Smith says, "Our difference make us uniquely interesting, but not unique. It's the same life force in each one of us."

The Human Race

It is vital to know *there is only one current human race*. Any differences in skin tones between black, white, brown, tan, are purely due to the amounts of melanin needed and evolutionarily developed to adapt to local doses of sunlight. Slight differences in leg bone structure are based on whether longer or stronger thigh bones were once needed for running in a jungle terrain because there were no roads for wheels. Differences in eyelid and nose shapes are adaptations for heat, cold, or desert winds—and so forth. Geographic isolation made some feature adaptations more dominant; intermarriage increased distinguishing features. There's no more to choose between these differences than between two cats, and only the mother cares.

And know we haven't been here long. Carl Sagan says in *Dragons of Eden*, if fifteen billion years of cosmic history, from the Big Bang to now, is represented by one year, our whole human history occurs in the last ten hours.

But "human evolution is the original revenge of the nerds," says Steven Pinker in his book *How the Mind Works*. We have no poisonous fangs, no great strength, speed, flight feathers, or even especially sensitive senses; in short, our bodies are no great shakes except for our thumbs. But essentially, it is not our bodies but our brains, "our behavior and the mental programs that organize it," that allows us humans to control the fate of a lion rather than the other way around. Pinker is saying that the nerds, not the jocks of the Earth, are currently in charge.

About 55 million years ago, the earliest primates looked like tarsiers and lemurs. These were the first nerds, with bigger brains in relation to their body size than most other animals, and more complex wiring. By 35 to 31 million years ago, there were lots of monkey-like creatures, and by 23 million years ago, East Africa was home to many kinds of hominoid primates, the superfamily to which we and the great apes—gibbons, orangutans, gorillas, chimps, and bonobos—belong. Genetic studies indicate a date of 6-7 million years ago as the time of divergence between the chimpanzee and us.

Carl Sagan, Louis Leakey, and many anthropologists and evolutionary biologists say that it was standing upright, the change in physical behavior, that changed the wiring of our brains. When we left the shrinking forests and emerged onto Africa's savannas about 4-5 million years ago, we stood upright more continuously to spot danger farther away. The Australopithecus afarensis known to the world as Lucy whose bones were found in East Africa is one of the mothers of our human race. (It is worth remembering in our color-conscious world that the first ancestors, the first human people, the first scientists, artists, kings, emperors, civilizations, were not white or yellow or pink. All our human ancestors were black. All humans come from the first 150,000 or so Africans who, seeking food, traveled north and spread out over the rest of the world. Every family on Earth, therefore, has black roots.)

So, standing up like Lucy to look for food and danger, our ancestors added to our opposable thumbs and frontal vision two more characteristics of the human race, and so altered our neuronal circuitry forever. First, standing upright fixed the human spine permanently in an upright position and freed the hands for tools and further technological development. This allowed the taming of fire, the cooking of meat that was easier to chew, that diminished jaw size and left more space for the brain. Even more startling than the effects of standing up and freeing the hands for tools was the second most important and dangerous development in the human brain. We could not fight predators larger and stronger than ourselves. *But our brains could form an image, remember it, and retreat for cover while the predator was still distant.* Memory and image-making are both necessary for passing on culture and technology. They are also the basis for the negative problems of our brains, like individual resentment, cultural hate, racism, and global war. But the point remains: *a change of behavior changes the brain.*

Our Brains Create Images

The brain's capacity to create and retain in long-term memory the images it forms may have saved our physical lives. We had to be able to tell the difference between a lion who would eat us, and a plant whose roots we could eat. But image-making is also the basis for 'self' and 'other'—

the origin of separation and loneliness. We are made of the same atoms as all matter. Image-making is for safety, and because, as evolutionary brain scientist Zoltan Torey says in his book *The Crucible of Consciousness*, if our brains had to "cope with the ocean of light waves, pressure waves, and assorted raw data in which it is immersed, it would be overwhelmed and unable to make sense of it." And along with images, unlike the brains of other animals so far as we know, our human brains developed language, spoken, written, electronically encoded. We can pass along our knowledge—but also our fears, prejudices, idiocies—to our children.

Freaks, Nerds, and How Evolution Works

Charles Darwin and Stephen Jay Gould are two of my favorite evolutionary scientists. And they are freaks, even among the nerds. My definition of a freak is a brain that can't help seeing the truth clearly right through its own inherited knowledge and cultural mud—and, equally, has the courage, knows the necessity, to speak up about it. Another word for this is genius. People like this are often jailed, crucified, burned at the stake, or at least politically and socially ostracized for their pains, especially when they offend the self-importance of the human race.

We once believed we lived on the central body of a limited universe until Copernicus, Galileo, and Newton, and eventually modern astrophysicists identified our Earth as a tiny satellite of an ordinary star at the edge of a small galaxy amid a cluster of galaxies among many galactic clusters in what might even be only one of many universes.

So much for the importance of Earth. As for the human beings on Earth, we are hardly a pinnacle.

• As Charles Darwin pointed out, we are simply a branch of the family of other great apes provably descended from the same primate ancestor, and we share 97%-99% of the same genetic material with our other ape cousins.

• Dr. Stephen Jay Gould writes in his *Full House*: "Darwin's revolution will be completed when we smash the pedestal of arrogance" and understand that life is nonpredictable and nondirectional, "recognizing that Homo sapiens…is a tiny twig, born just yesterday on an enormously arborescent tree of life that would never produce the same set of branches if regrown from seed. We grasp at the straw of progress…crave progress as our best hope for retaining human arrogance in an evolutionary world." *But evolution is only, by definition, change; it does not mean progress.*

• Darwin describes evolution in his *Origin of Species*:

  1. All organisms tend to produce more offspring than can possibly survive.

  2. Offspring vary among themselves—they are not carbon copies.

3. Some of this variation is passed down by inheritance to future generations. For principles of inheritance see heredity scientist Gregor Mendel's later principles of inheritance—and current genomics.

4. Survivors among the offspring will be those with the best adaptations to changing local environments. Adaptations that endure produce evolutionary change, and Darwin called this process *natural selection*. Again, this principle of natural selection has nothing to do with progress, as very often local adaptation may lead to simplification, not complexity. Certain extremely simple bacteria can kill a human being, or make us physically ill or mentally disordered.

Evolution for Humans is Only Partly in the Genes

As Gould says, we have biological potential, we are not completely biologically determined. And as Ratey points out, "genetics is not destiny."

The International Genome Project is mapping out 100,000 genes in the human genome, about 30,000 to 50,000 of which are designated for the brain. "But we must remember that genetics is not destiny. A mere 50,000 genes for the brain are not nearly enough to account for the 100 trillion synaptic connections that are made there." Genes may set some boundaries: two skinny, four-foot-tall parents aren't really the best candidates to give birth to a fullback. But within genetic boundaries there are enormous possibilities for variation. "Everything we do affects the activity of our genes," Ratey says. A child prodigy who practices plays a great piano; one who doesn't practice becomes a dud like the rest of us. Ratey's favorite mantras are 'wire by firing' and 'use it or lose it.' We are not set in cement.

As for environmental effects on destiny, these can be overcome just as genetic effects can be overcome, by changing behavior and attitudes and therefore the neurons' electrochemical transmissions in the brain's synapses. Short of flapping its arms to fly, the human being can rewire and map much of its own destiny.

The point is, we no longer have to wait for evolution to change the life of an individual brain. Now that we have a better understanding of how the brain works, we have some tools to change ourselves without waiting hundreds of thousands of years to mutate.

1. We have the technology to watch the brain's activity.

2. We have psychotherapy, with tests, diagnosis, and dialogue.

3. We have drug therapy to correct chemical imbalances in the body/brain.

4. We are learning to pay attention to the ways of the self in daily life, correcting our behavior as we go along.

As physicist Nancy Teasdale points out, "Evolution is a grand example of how behavior changes the brain. But with chemical therapy where necessary and personal behavior changes, we can now change biology during the timespan of a human life."

Ben and Jack: Genius; Dyslexia; ADD; Violence—in Siblings

It's not just what we get from genes and environment. It's what we do with all that equipment that makes us what we are.

Ben and Jack, in the same high school as Dana, Mike, and Claudia, suffer from their own set of problems.

Both brothers suffer from the brain and social difficulties presented by genius. They also suffer from the major disorders of dyslexia and attention deficit disorder, ADD. These are compounded, of course, by society's often malfunctioning educational system, not just teachers in schools but parents at home. Mostly, the system:

1. Fails to teach us about how our brains and bodies work, our history of animal aggression, and that because of our capacity (usually undeveloped) for intelligence, we need no longer be violent to survive. (If you see a man beating a child with a stick, of course you take away the stick. This is not the same as living in an armed and armored tank one's whole life.)

2. Emphasizes competition instead of cooperation to earn approval both in the classroom and out, both at home and in the world and to win the world.

Our society and malfunctioning educational system's values makes all of us emotionally ill, and frequently wrong. This creates violence in us all. Being aware of this means it isn't necessary to act it out. But if, added to faulty educational systems both in school and at home, neural networks in the brain are faultily wired, a person can be in and cause great trouble.

Ben and Jack's Problems

Dyslexia, according to Ratey, clinically encompasses a "wide range of language disorders. Some dyslexics have trouble processing sound, others have trouble processing the visual word, and still others find it difficult to extract meaning from printed words." About 20% of Americans could be diagnosed with dyslexia. Dyslexics are born with "several structural differences in their brains that make reading, sounding out words, or spelling extremely difficult," Ratey goes on, "despite their normal or above-average intelligence." Miswired nerve cells in the middle of pregnancy, scientists think, may account for dyslexics' difficulties in processing necessary visual and auditory input. They think the problem is linked both to the 6th and 7th chromosomes, and MRIs can image the activity in the appropriate areas of the brain. My point, again, is that the workings of the brain are physical. It should be pointed out that while scientists agree that the human brain is wired for language, we are not genetically prewired for reading and writing. Reading and writing are culturally transmitted, learned-in-every-lifetime behavior, and recent at that. Writing was only invented about 4,000 to 5,000 years ago, and reading, literacy, has only became popular in the last few centuries since the printing press was invented in the 15th century.

Attention Deficit Disorder is a syndrome of difficulties in paying attention at home and in school. According to the *Diagnostic and Statistical Manual of Mental Disorders, Fourth Edition (DSM-IV)*, people with this disorder find it hard to persist with the same task, the same relationship, or even remember whether they were sent to the store for milk or a pair of gloves. It is hard for them to follow through on anything, at school or at home or on the job. They have an aversion to organization, requests for attention, tasks that require sustained self-application, or anything that requires close attention, from homework to personal relationships to job paperwork. Works habits are messy, materials disorganized or missing. A major problem for people with ADD is distractibility. Irrelevant stimuli, the odd noise or event, and they are off-task. They are forgetful, in social situations seem not to be listening, not remember, not care what is being said or by whom. They are forgetful in daily activities, even of appointments necessary to their own welfare. They do not easily follow rules, remember the time, keep even to their own plans. They are not, in terms of this disorder, oppositional, though secondarily, oppositional defiant disorder (chronically angry, resentful, vindictive, unruly behavior) may follow. But people with ADD really just can't pay attention. Even sustained relationships to people, as to work, are difficult for them.

That being said, if someone with ADD is smart, talented, or has a particular interest, focus may be intense, and a particular talent addressed until perfected, like Ben's genius in football and Jack's genius with computers.

Both Ben and Jack had to deal with the learning disability called dyslexia. Because they were so bright, they invented ways of getting through school tests and reading assignments. They cheated when possible, bought answers when they could, used their nondyslexic girlfriends as crib sheets and tutors, and made use of special ed classes when they could not evade them in school. They felt both stupid and at the same time smarter than their friends for beating the system.

Ben and Jack are proof again that it's not just what we get from genes and environment, it's what we do with all that equipment that makes us what we are.

Ben's and Jack's Feelings

Two brothers under the age of ten are playing in their room when their mother enters screaming at them. "This room is a jungle. I told you to pick it up. The whole house is a mess. I can't cope any more. I wish I were dead. I wish I had never been born."

Jack's reaction is, "Mom is so miserable she wants to kill herself. It must be my fault. What awful thing have I done, what's wrong with me, to make my mom feel so bad?" He rushes to cling to her with a hug.

Ben's reaction is a shrug. "Mom is having a bad day. She'll pull out of it." And he puts away some toys, clothes, juice cartons, and goes back to his football video game.

Ben and Jack shared the same gene pool, had the same parents, grew up in the same environment. But their brains processed experience so differently in some ways, that their views of both parents and their home life—true of many siblings—presented different pictures. Simply put, their brains reacted differently to the same stimulus. For Jack, his mother's unhappiness was his fault and a source of lifelong guilt. For Ben, his mother was just having a bad day. Other people's problems had little to do with him.

By the age of seventeen, both stood out in school from the rest of their classmates, and both were highly, belligerently, competitive. Ben, big, muscled, fast, was a major football hero on the high school varsity. His dyslexia had not mattered to a major university, and he had already been awarded a football scholarship. Jack was a techie, brilliant in science and computers. He could take apart any machine from car to clock, make a dozen kinds of bombs. In Jack's field, his dyslexia did matter, however, and eventually he could not test well enough for a scholarship for his further education. Both boys were measurable geniuses. Genius means marked capacity and brain scientists list several kinds, among them music and math genius, natural sciences genius, art and verbal genius, and kinesthetic genius to which category dancers and natural athletes belong with their superb spatial/movement sense. Both boys also had as yet unmedicated ADD, attention deficit disorder.

Ben, with his physically violent competitiveness both on and off the football field, was often in trouble for fighting, for behaving like a loose cannon.

Whenever he was punished, in school by a teacher's discipline, at home by his father, he took a gleeful revenge by getting drunk and stealing—a car, a television set, money, bicycles—he didn't care. He decided if he couldn't get ahead by book learning, he could use his body skills better than anyone. Jack, as mentally competitive as his brother was physically competitive, had an equally violent fantasy life: with his room set up as a home lab, Jack built better and better bombs. He felt entitled to explode these from time to time to see if they worked, so far without serious injury to himself or anyone else. Both boys belonged to motorcycle gangs—clubs, they protested to their parents. Both had occasionally spent a night or two in the local jail. Both were attractive, especially to girls, and had not been without one girlfriend or another to have sex with since they were thirteen. In Jack's case, the relationships were sensitive and caring; in Ben's, it was all about his needs. For neither boy did any relationship last more than a few months or a year, though they had no clue why this was so.

Teen Problems in General

Let it be said here that the fact that all the teenagers in this book have big problems does not mean that all teenagers have the major problems that result from brain disorders.

All teens, however, have some problems. All teens face the extremely difficult developmental and cultural problems of adolescence, mainly:

1. Teens struggle with newly powerful surges of hormones, an energetic emotion system in the brain, and still under-developed prefrontal lobe circuits in areas of judgement and control.

2. Teens struggle with the family's biological urge to keep them safe, your equal biological urge for safety, another phrase for dependence, and your brain's newly develop-ing cortical equal and opposite requirements to function independently.

3. Teens struggle with the cultural demands that you begin to decide your career, even your marriage partner, before your prefrontal cortex has finally matured at the age of twenty (or later). The culture hands you increasingly com-plex information requirements and therefore educational years of preparation before you can make a decent living in the adult world. The culture gives you mixed messages about your body, brain, the purpose of your life, whether you belong to yourself or to THEM, and even which THEM that is. You've heard these mixed messages your whole life:

   - Be a good person—but climb over anybody you have to on your way up the ladder.

- Be fair—but make as much money as you can and keep as much as possible for you and yours.

- Be kind—but kick butt on the soccer field, on the job, and don't let anyone anywhere for any reason get the best of you.

- Don't judge—but know who the suckers are and let no one play you for a sucker.

- Everybody was created equal, except maybe THOSE PEOPLE, and we all know who THOSE are.

- Marry for love—but make sure whoever it is comes from money, social position, "sound" religious and political affiliation.

- Love everyone—but above all be loyal. Of course, the definition of loyal is tribalism: this is a diseased attitude that excludes other nationalities, beliefs, colors, even families. Anything that includes only some people excludes everyone else is the source of conflict that messes up our lives. But who tells teens this?

Add your own confusions about mixed messages to the list.

Assessment

Both Ben and Jack have the brain and social difficulties presented by genius, and the major disorders of dyslexia and attention deficit disorder. Ben's problem was auditory dyslexia. This left him unable to properly understand or follow through on directions. But when Ben was playing football or planning one of his stealing schemes, he had remarkable powers of concentration, almost an obsessive-compulsive quality. Almost any sport or subversive scheme that interested him, that gave him a high, made Ben concentrate enough to carry it through.

"Then I stopped being bored, restless, frustrated with rules I never understood, in a rage at being asked to understand what I couldn't, follow directions I couldn't follow. The constant mood swings stopped, the temper tantrums I had over every frustration stopped, the worry over procrastinating, the self-hate—everything stopped when I was doing something I could do well. I know I got compulsive about sports. Why not? I could do sports—and it was the only thing that made me feel good about myself. The only other thing I had going for me was being charming—I got good at being charming so people would excuse, forgive, or do for me what I couldn't do for myself. But sports! That I could do for myself."

Jack's dyslexia was compensated for by his natural genius in math and science. Friends got him through English and history, and since he didn't have auditory dyslexia like his brother, he could learn by listening over and over until test material was in his memory long enough to pass. His English and history marks were indifferent to bad, but Jack didn't care. He had his science, his computers, his bombs.

Rewiring

People are understandably troubled, an article in *U.S. News & World Report*, when they hear that "toddlers are getting thousands of prescriptions for stimulants, mood stabilizers, and antidepressants every year." Psychoactive drugs from Ritalin to Prozac to Wellbutrin and more are being administrated to children and adolescents. The American Academy of Child and Adolescent Psychiatry has insisted repeatedly that drug treatment should be part of a broader treatment program, but drug treatment is still highly controversial and sadly, there are seldom enough funds anyway. Also, of course, research in the mental diseases and emotional disorders of childhood must be as mandatory as it is for adults, but not enough is being done.

For Ben and Jack, proper diagnosis and drug therapy are necessary before the two of them start the third World War. But joining teen support groups for their specific disorders should be insisted on by equally supportive and understanding parents and teachers. And if they can't find support in school or at home, somewhere in their reading they must discover for themselves that they have to understand themselves and change the behavior that will rewire the neural networks in their brains. School tests, like childhood, will soon be over. They can begin their lives all over again as adults.

U.S. News & World Report says researchers show that emotionally troubled young people often end up in juvenile detention facilities rather than in treatment. Among the nearly two thousand offenders, boys and girls ages 10 to 18 held in a Chicago center, most had psychiatric disorders such as depression and ADD or drug and alcohol disorders. "It's not that these kids have criminal proclivities…but that kids get shunted into the criminal justice system because their treatment options have been cut."

Other factors that hinder recovery, as teacher Anna B. Smith says, are: 1) mental illness does not respond quickly to treatment and requires a patience teenagers often do not have; 2) the teen patient often rejects the prescribed treatment and prefers self-medication to any prescribed treatments; and 3) teen rage at parents, any authority, and 'the system' can blind teens to help. One teenager said that when her mother suggested she go to Alateen, she told her mother to go "fry ice."

The obvious lesson here is that in this overcrowded, speeding world, we can fall through the cracks, be misdiagnosed and misunderstood. So it really is up to each of us, the work of understanding ourselves and what is making each of us suffer. And it's up to each of us to stop reinforcing the suffering by stopping whatever behavior is causing the pain. No one else might be around to do it. No one else actually can do it.

And we're all in the same boat, each of us variations on the same human themes. Ben and Jack share everything— family and gene pool, even mental disorders. They turned out both alike and unique. As do we all.

CHAPTER SIX

Brains and Behavior
Talents and I.Q.—Personality and Problems—
The Problems of Misfits

The Secret of Life

When I was a teenager, I was absolutely certain that there was a key to living life, that I was missing that key, and that other people knew the secret I did not somehow share. When I grew older, I realized most people had no more clue to the secret of living a happy, connected life instead of a lonely, crazy one than I did. I wanted the secret of the joy of living and I wanted to learn what to do about its pains. I scrambled through life blindly. But I kept listening at keyholes. I was not interested in hand-me-down platitudes and second-hand knowledge. I was not interested in rules or following someone else's authority. I was interested in learning how to learn for myself. I did this by reading. I found thinkers who understood my question, and they all, from Socrates to Jesus to Buddha to Krishnamurti, from Freud to Stephen Hawking to Stephen Jay Gould, all of them seemed to say the same thing: self-knowledge is the key—since it's the self that's the problem, understanding your self (meaning to know your own conditioning—biological, species, family, cultural, personal background—some to enjoy, some to toss, but none of it to rule you), is the key to being free of the pains it causes you. A pain in the self can be a great teacher: the joy of getting beyond it, an even greater one. It even turns out self-knowledge is the basis for relationship and the end of loneliness.

Personalities and the Problems They Can Cause

Not all problems mean something is wrong with us. Sometimes, the problem is simply that what we are upsets other people. Just as some people are not your type, you may not be theirs. Fear of difference and jealousy over supposed or actual superiority are the biggest problems. Talent and smart brains are tremendous gifts from the gods: they can also make you feel different and very lonely, writing about, painting, studying life under a microscope instead of living it. Talent can make your brain so specialized that it cuts you off from other people and the intelligence of living the whole of your life. Individual human awareness seems happier when connected to all human awareness, and so it is with talent: it seems to need to be used properly for the greater human good, not as a self-serving instrument, or you'll pay a price in isolation and spite.

Sometimes a price is paid anyway, in other people's jealousy or fear of your talent and knowledge, of what you discover—scientists like Galileo found that out. We may all be created equal under the law, but it is not true we were all created equal by nature. If you think of yourself as just plain lucky, not something special—if you think of your talent as a gift you were given instead of a superior attribute—you'll suffer less lonely arrogance. And it's always worth remembering that smarts aren't necessarily the best of nature's survival skills.

"Intelligence is much greater than intellect, for it is the integration of reason and love; but there can be intelligence only when there is self-knowledge, the deep understanding of the total process of oneself," Krishnamurti says in *Education and the Significance of Life*.

It is only when thoughts, talents, and all the busyness of consciousness shuts up and stays quiet that awareness of the whole of life, and the glory of its connections, can take place. Talent and being smart can, in other words, get in the way of intelligence.

That being said, and it being understood that talent and extra brain circuits can exact a price, can make you lopsided and a leper, having them can be a lot of fun. Tiger Woods, whose kinesthetic genius actually sees more and better than the rest of us, seems to be having a very good time.

Talented brains are not only differently wired, they actually look different when activated and scanned from ordinary brains. And while genius brains and especially talented brains may function in their specialized areas in more spectacular ways than the usual, they may suffer equally spectacular deficits, from social disabilities to Tourette's tics to mental disorders to simple problems in judgement like coming in out of the rain. Temple Grandin, autistic, invented specially engineered ramps so that for cattle, slaughter is less terrifying. Psychiatrist Oliver Sachs described a talented surgeon and pilot, with severe Tourette's tics, except during operations and when he was flying his own plane. The artist Van Gogh, whose paintings are now among the most sought after in the history of art, was institutionalized for schizophrenia. Einstein was dyslexic; Mozart, bipolar.

A reminder about talented brains: The study of ants by Deborah Gordon, in *The Best American Science Writing 2000*, reminds us that it takes more than a talented teenager's brain alone to make a success. There are three distinct levels that determine an ant's behavior: the ant itself, its colony, its population. These affect both individual achievement and the achievement of the population as a whole.

Talent takes 1) mentoring; 2) opportunity; and 3) society's blessing to succeed. In the old days, a talented female Shakespeare would not have been taught to read, never mind allowed to act on a stage. A talented female Michelangelo would have been stuck beating laundry on a rock. Even these days, teenagers who are female, black, brown—or inner-city-schooled and poor—may not receive enough mentoring, opportunity, or approval to bloom.

Writer's Brain

The writer Stephen Hall, in his article *Journey to the Center of My Mind* (*New York Times Magazine, Best American Science Writing 2000*), was a test subject for MRI, magnetic resonance imaging, to take pictures of his brain as he went through his writing process. "There, in a three-pound pudding of neurons and wiring, lie the keys to the kingdoms of memory, of thought, of desire, of fear, of the habits and skills that add up to who we each are...I realize...there is no center of activity, only waystations in a circuit...churning in some mysterious neural communion. And the notion of mind? Perhaps it's nothing more than the heat given off by our personalized circuits, everywhere and nowhere."

In one test, Hall was given ten seconds to tell a little story in his head in response to a series of pictures, visual prompts. His basic language centers, in a small patch of cortex on the left side called Broca's area, lighted up. If the architecture of every brain is pretty much the same, the pictures in it vary according to the memories synaptically stored all over the

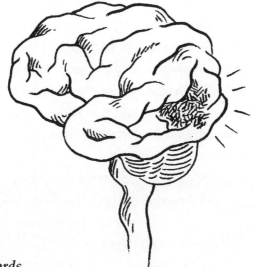

Seeing Words

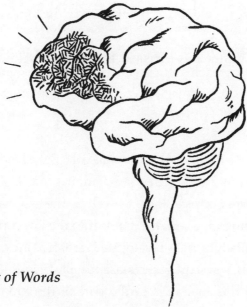

Thinking of Words

brain's gray cell matter. You use short-term or working memory for thinking and problem-solving. This allows you to carry on a conversation using your short-term memory and still use long-term memory for remembering your name.

In a writer's brain, not only the language centers but the visual and aural centers light up at cues, using two related capabilities on either side of the brain—one to create the stories using the right side of the brain, and the other to articulate them in speech on the left side. The hippocampus, thought to be involved in long-term memory, also lights up. But always, the story-telling areas are the most active, particularly the interior frontal gyrus.

So, while language for most, about 90% of us, primarily resides in the left hemisphere, the practice of the art of writing, storytelling, over and over again, exercises, muscularizes, a whole group of areas in the brain that work together.

Being a writer is as physical, as neurobiological, as being an athlete.

Artist's Brain

In the artist's brain, it is the visual cortex that lights up on the PET scans Restak uses for demonstration. The visual cortex, in the occipital lobe, as well as the association area for visual memory, which extends into the lower part of the temporal lobe, are well-developed in artists as are other parts of the sensory system. Artists use receptors near the body's surface, in this case cells in the part of the eye called the retina, to take in information from the environment. Again, it is good to remember that connections that are used are kept, as LeDoux says, and those that are unused are eliminated. This means that sight involves memory/knowledge as well as senses: people who have never seen before and whose eyes are restored to use by new technology may lack depth perception and visual experience. They may be unable to withstand the confusion of sudden sight. Documented cases show the occasional recipient of sudden sight to refuse what we think of as a gift and continue to live with eyes closed.

As for writers, actors, and athletes, it is in the continued practice of their talents that their genius thrives.

Motivation or Mental Illness?

With all our ideas about what it takes for a writer, actor, or an artist, a musician, a scientist, an athlete, to exercise her or his genius, there are still many unanswered questions about talent and what it is. We still haven't got answers to questions like, what is life? We really still don't know exactly what made some chemicals remain inert and some chemical molecules 3.8 billion years ago form the first bacteria we call life. And what is consciousness? We don't really know the answer to that, either. And we still haven't solved the riddle of talent. What makes a saint like Mother Teresa or a star like Elvis Presley? One school of thought calls these driven geniuses high in motivational energy. Another more behaviorist school calls the exceptionally bright and talented a bunch of addicts driven to perform over and over again by reward and punishment. And I know of a group of perfectly serious psychiatrists who refer to this component of genius's need to keep at it an obsessive-compulsive mental illness. In short, we just don't know how to assess genius and talent.

Working Memory

Working short-term memory is what makes us most human, says LeDoux. "In addition to helping us function from one moment to the next, working memory...registers our current activity while retrieving information from long-term memory...holding it at the ready. It is the mental glue that holds multiple connections together as we think a thought or enact an act, from beginning to end." One advantage to good working memory (disordered in people with ADHD or Alzheimer's) is that it can predict the consequences of our actions.

Working memory processes sensory inputs, problem-solves, relays information to long-term memory. Basic types of memory—sensory, motor, visuospatial, and language—give us sound, sight, taste, smell, touch, so our memories can be recalled from all sorts of sensory cues, and mental/motor tasks can be repeated. Dancers and athletes understand particularly about body memory.

Good memory is based on good learning in everyday experience.

Music and Lyrics and Motor Brains

Fine motor control of our vocal chords plus repetition of correct sounds gives us speech, song, music. The cerebellum plays a part in motor memory. For motor memories, the frontal cortex plans and organizes, while the basal ganglia and hippocampus act together to store long-term memory. Artistic individuals possess high levels of interhemispheric communication between right and left halves of the brain. Motor memory among musicians and athletes is achieved by a sophisticated feedback system that detects errors made as the movement is learned. For a piano-player the main motor regions are brain areas that control the eyes for reading the music, the ears for listening to sounds, and the fingers for manipulating the keys. In the second stage, additional neurons refine the critical neural firing patterns—which is why practice makes perfect. Motor memory and skill-learning are intimately related for athletes as well. Like any other higher cognitive skill such as language or emotion, motor memory occurs in areas all over the brain, coordinated by the frontal lobe. Music and sports exercise the entire brain just as painting and writing do. In humans, language is the basic tool for forming memories and communicating culture down the generations, and language was possible only when the brain developed connections between higher-order motor and sensory areas and the frontal cortex so we could evolve naming things for a working memory system.

Division of Labor in the Cortex

What lights up in science geniuses, including math whiz-zes, techies, wonks and nerds of all kinds from Alan Turing to Richard Feynman, Albert Einstein to Bill Gates, is a combination of all the areas above. Every cortex, all the substructures of the brain, fire all the time. As Stephen Pinker says in *How the Mind Works*, "creative geniuses are distinguished not just by their extraordinary works but by their extraordinary way of working."

ALL THE TIME!

"Geniuses…may also have been dealt a genetic hand with four aces. But they are not freaks with minds utterly unlike ours….The genius creates good ideas because we all create

BRAINS AND BEHAVIOR

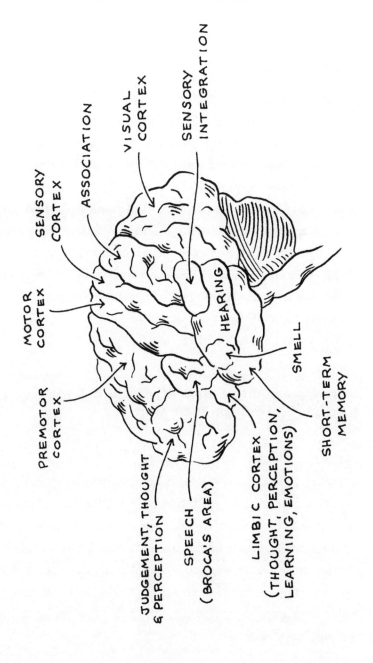

good ideas; that is what our combinatorial, adapted minds are for."

There is one low-grade genius I know intimately. I would describe her as a talented, hard-working, obsessive, self-absorbed, socially disabled, and inner-directed compulsive, self-propelled towards posterity if current esteem fails.

Geniuses are talented people who work hard, who practice, who have enough drive to absorb early rejection—it takes most talented people about ten years to do their first really good work—and who, while they care what people think of their work, never let disapproval stop them from doing what they do, over and over again.

As Maya Angelou once said, being a writer comes no more naturally than being a brain surgeon.

You want to be good? Practice. Get good.

More Personalities that Attract Problems through No Fault of Their Own

Marion

Marion's parents had just told her they were getting a divorce. What had at first felt like a shock to the safe, comforting nest with its unchanging cycle of routines—daily family dinners, yearly birthdays and Christmases, family vacations to islands in the sun—was also felt by Marion to be something of a relief. Her parents quarreled all the time now. Bitter words and accusations lately filled a home once loving and respectful.

Marion, at fourteen, was scared: about her future; about her loyalties to each of her parents; about what some of her friends would think; and about her own feelings of anger and guilt. She went from being mad at her parents and blaming them for the misery they were causing her to feel, to feeling guilty in case she herself was the cause of their misery and quarrels. Marion felt even more guilty because she had a secret. It was a secret that was enough to make any two parents quarrel to the point of divorce. If her parents were quarreling because they had guessed her secret, the family's entire unhappiness might all be her fault.

Divorce itself wasn't the end of the world. She knew that. She had friends at school who lived with one parent and visited the other on weekends. Some already had step-fathers and step-mothers, or suffered through a series of live-in lovers. What was going to get her in trouble at school, what was going to lose Marion her friends, her popularity, was the same secret that might be the cause of her parents' fights.

Within a month, Marion's parents separated. Her father moved to a condominium. Her mother went to stay with one of her women friends with plenty of space on her farm. Marion spent half the week in her father's town apartment. She spent half the week feeding chickens. Within a couple of months, her father had begun to date other women.

"When are you going to start dating, mom?" Marion asked.

"I'm already living with my partner," said Marion's mother. "Darling, I'm gay. I'm a lesbian."

"But that's my secret," said Marion. "I'm gay."

"I know, dear. So is your Uncle Harry. Runs in the family biological pool."

"But what do I do? How do I live?" Marion wailed.

"You can start by remembering that if there is a problem, it's other people's, not yours," said her mother simply. "Some people have blue eyes. Some people are gay."

Charlie

Charlie's parents were different colors, and he was born with the best of both of their features: he was beautiful, smart, gifted, and charming—like so many biracial children, he had strengths from several cultures. After all, inbreeding does not bring out the best in the human race.

Before he went to school, Charlie had no idea he was different from anybody else, and because he came from a mixed family with brown, white, and black grandmothers, black, white, and brown cousins, he thought the whole world was equally varied. When he was six, and in the first grade, he discovered the hard fact: white children had parents who didn't like the fact that Charlie was half black; black parents didn't like the fact that Charlie was half white. Since children have to be taught racism—we are not born with this quality—some parents seized Charlie for their first lesson.

One day during play period, the two boys in Charlie's class who liked him best invited Charlie to play Civil War with them. One boy was the North, the other was the South.

"And you be the slave because that's what black people are," they said to Charlie.

The fact that Charlie's grandma, who happened to be a well-known author, marched on the school the next day demanding to teach that first grade the evolution/anthropology lesson they would never forget—about how we are all black, all descended from the first black African human beings—did not erase from Charlie's six-year-old brain his first realization that through no fault of his own, he had a problem.

The Effect on the Brain of Being Treated Like a Misfit

Humans, like wolves, are pack animals, social animals. For survival, we live in tribes. The consequence of being left out of the tribal family, the pack, is death. Watch any *National Geographic* film on animals from zebras to chimpanzees to the suffering of our own human orphaned creatures, and you will see them being eaten for lunch by the lions or wasting away from loneliness or developing any number of stress disorders.

To treat any human being as outsiders, as not having a place in the pack, is to give their brains a fright. Our ancient brain centers tell us that to be left out is to die. This scares the daylights out of us. "Evolution," says Restak, "has designed the brain so that a frightening stimulus [explosion, runaway car, terrorism, crime, abuse, racism, group rejection] is picked up by the thalamus and sent directly to the amygdala…which, in turn, communicates with the brain stem to set in motion the body's 'fight-or-flight' responses." This is useful in life and death situations, but to live a daily life in a state of fear and anxiety produces personality problems that can last a lifetime. Freezing for a few seconds until your cerebral cortex works out whether a male shadow on the wall is a friend or a rapist, whether an empty beach or shadowy street is safe, may save your life. On the other hand, if every shadow every day is perceived as a threat, and your amygdala always overrides your cortex so you live in a constant state of emotional arousal, you can make yourself psychologically very sick. Disorders like PTSD (post-traumatic stress disorder, the "most dramatic example of the fear response gone awry" as Restak calls it), or crippling varieties of the ordinary stresses of life such as public speaking, depression, phobias—all this can create high levels of stress hormones—principally cortisol, secreted by the adrenal glands. The adrenal glands are located near the kidneys, not in or near the brain. But it is the brain that controls their secretions. There is a chemical within the brain, corticotropin-releasing factor (CRF for short) that neuroscientist Charles Nemeroff describes as controlling not only cortisol secretion but levels of norepinephrine, a second stress-related hormone.

The point here is that, while physical fear and its chemical urges are necessary to get out of the way of an actual speeding train coming at you, too much psychological stress too constantly is damaging to the system.

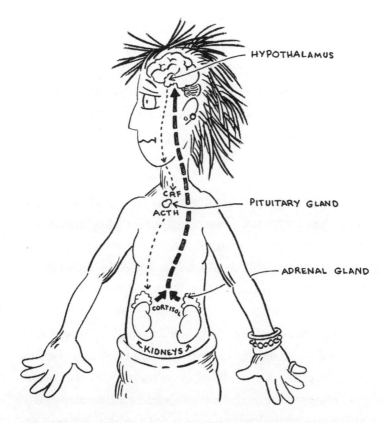

Anxiety and panic attacks, sleep, appetite, mood disorders, to say nothing of aggressive behavior disorders (whether in the revenge/attention-getting overachiever or underachieving bully), can result from society's rejection of a human being and the subsequent stress hormonal imbalances that can follow. The point here is that if you sometimes find that brainy, gifted, gay, differently colored or abled people grow up to behave oddly, *their disturbances may not be inborn but due only to their reactions to our suspicious treatment of them.*

Surviving Adolescence Well

We all get older if we don't get dead. We survive the teenage years sooner or later and find ourselves by twenty or twenty-one launched into the world of college, the services, marriage, jobs, careers, all that. Whether we actually mature enough to handle all this properly or not is based on two basic conditions.

1. Proper biophysical development of the body and especially the prefrontal cortex, the CEO of our judgement, plans, behaviors, decisions, moral and ethical positions, allows us to control impulses, measure consequences, and live to good purpose.

2. Paying close attention to the conditioned, knee-jerk reactions of thought and feeling and behavior and learning to stop at the source whatever will hurt ourselves or others. The conditioned thoughts and feelings may not go away, but maturity is based on not acting them out, and on behavior that is good for all, not just for the self.

You can decide whether to become one of those tragic infantile adults who blame and whine, abuse sex or drugs or children, yell, hurt other people whenever they get frightened or upset; or to be happy. It's freeing to know it isn't what cards you're dealt that decides your life, it's what you understand about the game and how you play it.

CHAPTER SEVEN

All Human Beings Feel Lonely and Scared
Some Are Damaged—Some Are Mentally Ill— More Teen Stories

If someone asked you, "What is life?" what would you say? Wouldn't you say that life is everything you do outwardly, go to school, play sports, go to clubs or parties, work if you have a job or do chores at home, spend time with your friends—all that. And also there is your inward life, thinking, feeling, dreaming, having the intelligence to observe your behavior, thoughts, dreams, nature, God and the universe if you are blessed to feel connection to all its music. Life is all that, isn't it, the outward and the inward?

But in human life (so far as we know, bacteria and stones don't suffer it) there is one really huge problem.

Because of our brain's imaging system, we survive; we can tell the difference between a bear and a bat. But those images also separate us, from each other, from nature, from the stars. Instead of feeling part of we feel different from and separate from all the other atoms in the universe. So our brain's skill at creating images is both our best survival skill and the very thing that makes all human beings feel separate, and therefore lonely and scared.

Because most people are never taught how the human brain works, our brains scare us. We never learn that:

1. The normal condition of the mind is to be empty and we get so frightened at the emptiness we fill it with all kinds of destructive escapes.

2. We invent a self, like a package with all its contents, to fill up the emptiness—and then believe in it and get upset when every few seconds the normal emptiness comes back.

In short, we frighten ourselves. So, while this chapter is going to deal with actual mental disorder and brain damage, it is also true that most of us at times display symptoms of mental illness or patterns of behavior beyond the "normal" range due to all the fear and loneliness that is part of just having a human brain. *It is only when bizarre patterns continue to disrupt or threaten our own lives or the lives of others that true mental illness exists and needs treatment. Mental disorder is truly physical illness, and must be given the same medical attention as a broken leg.*

As you read this chapter, don't be surprised if you start to think you have some or all of the symptoms described. It's only if symptoms persist and really interfere with your life that you are actually in trouble. We all exhibit "abnormal" or "unaverage" behavior sometimes. The person who is shy and withdrawn at a party is exhibiting the same form of behavior as the schizophrenic patient curled up against a hospital wall. The difference is that reasonably mentally healthy people bounce back from stress, do not lose touch entirely or for long periods of time with reality, and go on with their lives. *It really is a matter of degree, and we are sometimes all to some extent emotionally, cognitively, or mentally ill.*

Mental Health

The most basic definition of a mentally healthy person is one whose psyche can cope with internal and external reality well enough to get through life without harming itself or anyone else, or suffering so much that ordinary functioning in relationship to yourself, other people, and your work is disrupted. The ability to handle nondestructively whatever stress life hands you is the mark of a mentally healthy person. "Don't hurt" is a healthy mantra.

This does not mean you don't feel and act nuts for periods of time, or have depressions, or have murder and mayhem in your heart, or just simply quietly withdraw from the world. But if, whatever you feel, you can still get through class, wash the dishes and your face without killing yourself or anybody else, you're probably all right.

Because so many of us are partly or occasionally immature, under-developed in parts of our brains, or badly wired for any reason (with one hundred billion brain cells, a lot can go wrong), extreme cases like criminals, the psychotic, those with mental retardation or visible damage like Tourette's tics or cerebral palsy, make some people nervous. So we tend to put these people in prisons and asylums to hide them away. We do this partly to protect ourselves from the sociopaths without conscience, but also because we know we are all capable of their behavior to some degree and we don't want to be reminded. It is not always easy to stay sane in an insane world, and we don't want to see what can happen to the human brain out of control.

Mental Illness

As Hannah Carlson says in her book *I Have a Friend with Mental Illness*, "Mental illness is not fun—ever. To someone who has a mental illness, life can sometimes be a nightmare, often terrifying and bizarre, always a prison of isolation." Mental illnesses involve disorders of thinking, feeling, judgement, and behavior. Mental illnesses, like other illnesses, are diagnosed by their symptoms. *The Diagnostic Statistical*

Manual-IV (DSM-IV) is the recognized manual psychiatrists and psychologists use to diagnose mental illnesses. Some of the most common mental illnesses are grouped into:

- schizophrenia and other psychotic disorders
- mood disorders
- personality disorders
- anxiety disorders
- dissociative disorders

Most kinds of true mental illness can be physically seen through the use of PET scans and MRI.

Schizophrenia

Peter, like his friend and classmate Marion, had a secret. But Peter's secret, unlike Marion's, was serious enough to ruin his life. Like most teenagers, he kept the secret from the adult world as long as he could. He had begun to have trouble focusing and thinking clearly. He had begun to lose all his sense of fun, his connection to his friends. He had always been a good athlete and a good student; but strange voices, not his own, were now interfering with sports and studies. When he began to see devils' masks and black holes in his family's and friends' faces, he understood what was happening to him from what he had been learning in psychology class. Peter knew he had schizophrenia. It would not be long before his whole personality disintegrated, and he needed medication.

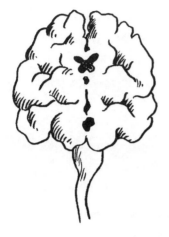

NORMAL

SCHIZOPHRENIA
(ENLARGED VENTRICLES)

Schizophrenia affects 300,000 Americans every year. Neuroscientist Elaine Walker states: "Schizophrenia originates from a brain abnormality located beneath the cortex, involving the [irregular transmission of the] neurotransmitter dopamine. This abnormality remains relatively silent until adolescence." MRI scans show that Peter's limbic, emotional, centers are also affected. The results are not only bizarre thoughts and beliefs (of being God or the C.I.A., of being persecuted or poisoned), but depression, lack of motivation, lack of emotional response to people and situations. Current medications still have some uncomfortable side effects, but with their use disorientation, hallucinations, and suicidal depression can be kept under control.

Mood Disorders

Major Depression. Anyone can suffer situational depressions. Family death, divorce, the loss of a boyfriend or girlfriend, moving to a strange town, getting bad marks, or not making a club or team—just going through adolescence with all its hormonal changes—can cause mood swings.

But major depression, the kind that Dana was trying to self-medicate by falling in love, and later with alcohol, although it can be triggered by loss, may last months or years and is not situational. It is a biochemical, physical syndrome (a collection of symptoms), a brain disease resulting from a chemical-neurotransmitter-imbalance involving the cerebral cortex, the amygdala, the hippocampus, the hypothalamus, and more. Neuroscientists are still not precisely certain about the chemistry that causes the dark nightmare that is depression. And not all depressions present exactly the same symptoms: there can be loss of appetite or increased eating; sleeping all the time or being unable to sleep; agitation and restlessness or profound inactivity; too little sex drive or sexual overdrive; headaches, digestive disorders, chronic pain. But all depressions carry sadness, feelings of hopelessness, suicidal ideas, guilt, worthlessness, despair.

PET scans show underactivity in the reality-evaluating frontal lobes and overdrive in the areas of the brain that process emotion. People like Dana whose brains are chemically imbalanced need diagnosis and treatment with one of the modern drugs now available such as Prozac, Zoloft, Paxil, and their like, as well as counseling.

Manic Depression or Bipolar Disorder. The same feelings of depression as above will alternate with mood highs so giddy that people with this up/down disorder will feel and behave as strangely during the high swing as the low. They are not just moody people: they, too, are chemically imbalanced and need to understand they have a mental illness. People with manic-depression have tremendous energy during their manic periods, talk fast, move fast, need little sleep, are hyperactive, unrestrained, impulsive, do everything to excess. They may spend too much money too fast, fall in love too much, take risks of all kinds, end up in trouble, even in jail or in the hospital. Manic depression can now also be treated with a drug such as Depacote.

Personality Disorders

As Hannah Carlson says in her book *Living with Disabilities*, "These disorders are characterized by a lifetime of conflict and distress. The pain is in the faulty perception of the self and relationships with others. It is based in the faulty wiring of the brain circuits due to variables that include both genetic and environmental influences."

Borderline Personality. This disorder manifests itself in relationships. People who have borderline personalities will do anything to avoid real or imagined abandonment. Their relationships with others are unstable, one minute desperately needy, the next rejecting. This is due to their own seesawing view of themselves, from self-critical to self-inflated importance. They have few inner resources, may self-mutilate or be suicidal, display rage, impulsivity, or antisocial behaviors. Teenagers may show many of these symptoms during various stages of adolescence, but these will pass with developmental maturation of the prefrontal cortex.

Obsessive-Compulsive Personality. Obsessive-compulsives are preoccupied with seemingly senseless thoughts and routines that intrude into and interrupt their daily activities. Joe does not dare sleep without checking the locks on his windows and all the doors to his house not just once, but many times throughout the night. Anne is so afraid of germs, she washes not only her hands but the dishes she uses over and over again. But what Joe and Anne have confided to each other is that the worst of all are their repetitive thoughts. Repetitive lock-checking, list-making, washing, bedtime routines bother them, but not as much as the repetitive thoughts, phrases, and fantasies in their heads. And in all its forms, these routines and thought patterns can become so overwhelming that they consume most or all of the day and interfere with school, jobs, family, and social life, isolating the person with this disorder in his or her own distress. Addiction to drugs, alcohol, shopping, gambling, eating, exercise, work—all are forms of obsessive-compulsive disorder. Therapy and drug therapy are required, as obsessive-compulsive disorder is a brain disorder, not just a character or personality flaw.

Anxiety Disorders. People with anxiety disorders cannot control their worrying. Distressing thoughts consume their attention and energy. They may worry about their own well-being or displace their anxiety onto worries about the family or animals or the world, not occasionally like the rest of us, but chronically until they are exhausted. PET scans show less activity in the prefrontal cortex, high activity in the amygdala and whole limbic system that processes emotions. Anxiety is a stress reaction, releasing too much adrenaline as well. Cognitive, or talk, therapy can rewire the brain's circuits with new behaviors and responses, together with drugs to block the physiological stress response.

ALL HUMAN BEINGS FEEL LONELY AND SCARED

Post-Traumatic Stress Disorder (PTSD) is a severe form of anxiety disorder afflicting people who have experienced or witnessed a terrifying event: crime, family violence, war, rape, terrorism, death, or torture. It is found in children and teenagers, and young adults especially who have experienced abuse or been exposed to abuse of others. It affects the same areas in the brain as anxiety disorder, and must be diagnosed and treated.

Phobias include abnormal fears of heights (acrophobia), small spaces (claustrophobia), open spaces (agoraphobia), darkness, certain animals, even people, combined with the terror of being caught someplace where the sufferer cannot escape easily. Phobics then experience panic attacks (heart racing, difficulty with breathing, sweats, dizziness). We all experience an occasional phobic response, the anxiety of being caught where we don't want to be, but for phobics, the feelings are always present.

Dissociative Disorders
Dissociative Amnesia. After a traumatic or intensely stressful event, people may defend their minds from the painful memory by forgetting who they are or any other personal information. This illness brings frightening confusion, disconnection to their own lives.

Dissociative Identity Disorder. Known once as multiple personality disorder, this manifests itself as two or more identities or personalities that take control of the behavior of one person. It is often people who have suffered severe physical or sexual abuse as children who suffer this disorder. Sometimes the personalities do not know of each other, sometimes one controls or endangers the others or even other people. A single psyche has invented other personalities to escape feeling the suffered abuse of the original personality.

Causes of Mental Illness

Most neuroscientists, psychologists, psychiatrists, and social workers report that the causes of mental illnesses involve a combination of neurochemical, physiological, psychological, and social factors. Particular genes, structures, or chemicals in the brain combined with social and environmental influences as well as the personal experience of those influences are the basis for the development of mental disorders. But many of these can be treated, and the work each of us does individually on our own behaviors to rewire our brain's circuits can make the difference between recovery and perpetuating illness.

Psychotic symptoms have been linked with other medical disorders, such as brain tumors, temporal lobe epilepsy, multiple sclerosis, sarcoidosis, Huntington's disease, cerebral vascular accidents (strokes), and AIDS, to name a few.

There are environmental causes for mental disorders, ranging from chemicals released into the air, soil, or food, the mother's use of drugs and alcohol during pregnancy, to malnutrition and physical neglect or abuse of children, or the witnessing of abuse in childhood as in the case of Holocaust survivors, American slavery and prejudice victims, even in second and third generation survivors, in Vietnam war and other war veterans, victims of incest, victims of homelessness and poverty and crime.

But it is possible not only to survive mental illness but thrive. We can do it with the right attitudes, the right therapies, the right medications, and most of all understanding about the way the brain works, the ways it has been and continues to be programmed every day by the society and the media we create. Most of all, we need to understand that our own brains can change our behavior, even among those of us who are mentally ill.

Drug Addiction and Brain Damage

Drug and alcohol abuse are perfect examples of how changing our behavior rewires our brains. As Restak says, "When a person takes an addictive drug, a massive surge of dopamine takes place within the pleasure circuits…far in excess of what occurs when the person experiences a normally positive event like winning in a sports competition….The surge is so great that it even eclipses the pleasure of orgasm." Obviously, the brain wants it again and again. The trouble is, this drug-associated chemical firing of the reward pathways of the brain kidnaps these pathways, while the other pathways in the brain necessary to living a rich, full life of relationships and meaningful work wither away like the muscles of paralyzed legs.

Drug abuse, whether alcohol, dexedrine, LSD, Ecstasy, heroin, cocaine, nicotine, or any others, can cause psychotic behaviors and permanent brain damage. Alcoholism and drug addiction may be genetically programmed in the same way as any chemical imbalance in the brain from depression to schizophrenia. The trouble with alcoholism and drug addiction is that you don't know you're chemically imbalanced until it is sometimes too late and your brain is already hooked. The pressured teenager may start with a little grass borrowed from a friend. She may do a little coke, try Ecstasy once at a rave, pop an upper at a club, an amphetamine, a downer, a barbiturate, experiment with hashish, morphine, mushrooms, inhalants. Her boyfriend might experiment with whatever is available in his parents medicine cabinet—pharmaceutical drugs are as available as street drugs. The more you take, the more your brain craves, and you're hooked. Not only does drug dependency torture the mind and body with the repeated round of craving and withdrawal symptoms, but it involves the teenage user in crime—theft, prostitution, the humiliations teens suffer during arrest and prison—to procure drugs and drug money.

Be afraid of drug use. Be careful with alcohol. The trouble with addiction is addiction. The brain never lets it end.

ALL HUMAN BEINGS FEEL LONELY AND SCARED

Brain Damage: Heredity, Accident, Disease

There are many ways brain tissue can be damaged, causing mental retardation, psychotic behavior, physical deformities, paralysis, spastic problems, seizures, blindness, early death. Children and teenagers with brain damage, whether hereditary, or caused by accident, tumors, disease, should be diagnosed as early as possible, cared for and taught as much as possible. The brain remains far more plastic and adaptable in youth than it does as it grows older.

There is the famous case of Harrison, a child with epilepsy who suffered so many seizures during the course of a day he lived in constant danger. His parents agreed to have the entire left side of his brain removed. With proper therapy, his right brain took over left-brain speech functions and the functioning of the right half of his body. This operation is less feasible for an adult because the brain of an adult is less adaptable than that of a child or a teenager. The connections between brain cells continue to alter all our lives, for as long as we live. The brain wires itself with each new experience, and reinforced connections are strengthened.

Causes and Effects of Brain Damage

In *I Have a Friend with Mental Retardation*, Hannah Carlson says, "People can be born with or acquire mental retardation in a variety of ways. Physical disorders or syndromes may accompany mental retardation...and...can cause defects in formation and function of...spine and brain development."

There are hereditary factors that can cause malformed brains: chemical imbalances, chromosomal disorders, skin and nerve disorders, muscular, craniofacial, skeletal disorders, developmental disorders of brain and spine formation like spina bifida. There can be complications during pregnancy such as Rh factors, or drug addiction in the mother, syphilis, X-ray of pregnant uterus, drugs like thalidomide, diseases a mother contracts during the first few months of pregnancy such as German measles, or malnutrition. Some of the results are absence of part of brain tissue, microcephaly (abnormally small brain and head formation), hydrocephaly (too much fluid pressing on and eventually shrinking the brain until it stops functioning, often causing early death). There is Down's Syndrome, not hereditary, but due to damage inside the womb. There are problems in and around labor and delivery, infections after birth like meningitis. There can be head injuries, accidents or abuse, infections like encephalitis, degenerative disorders like Parkinson's disease, seizure disorders, and so on.

Finally, there are the unknown causes for cases of mental retardation which have as yet no identifiable cause. And there are behavior patterns with as yet undetermined causes like autism, learning, and social disabilities.

Among older people, Alzheimer's disease, diseases such as arteriosclerosis and strokes, and senility—just plain getting old with the gradual failure of memory and motor circuit function in brain and body. For teens who love their grandparents, senility is not inevitable if the genes and environment permit, and if people stay physically and mentally active. Senility can also range from mild, even funny, to great loss and a vegetable-like state.

Head injuries from falls, crashes, blows, can happen at all ages, and the results can range from mild and transient to serious and permanent brain damage.

Such organic brain disorders are either acute (they happen suddenly and there is hope for recovery) or chronic (disorders develop more slowly and progressively get worse). The treatment and care of people with brain damage consists of repairing the physical damage where possible, and the use of behavior therapy to rewire the brain's circuits either for progress or for acceptance of new limitations or both. We never lose the ability to learn, and learning changes the patterns of brain activity.

It is vital to remember that what we call psychological problems and suffering are as physical as pneumonia or a broken arm, as they are rooted in the physical brain and nervous and hormonal systems.

SECTION TWO

Human Nature:
How We Got This Way

CHAPTER EIGHT

Why We Behave as We Do: Ages and Stages—Brain Parts and Maps

How Our Brain Circuits Get Wired—Genes and Environment

What Is Learning? What Is Memory?

Learning is input. It is the transmission of experience along your flexible synaptic circuits, rewiring the circuits when required. Memory is stored learning. Some learning stored as memory is evolutionary, genetic (like the need to eat to stay alive, or the need for life to reproduce itself). Some learning stored as memory you've acquired from the womb, through babyhood, throughout the prolonged childhood and adolescence of human beings (not just to eat, but what is good to eat, not just to reproduce but with whom to mate).

To review, the nervous system is made up of brain, spinal cord, and nerves. This is the body's electrochemical communications system, sending chemical signals as electrical impulses from the body to the brain and from the brain throughout the body. The brain receives information in various ways: externally through the body's five sense organs; eyes, ears, nose, tongue and palate, skin. It receives information through experience, instruction, physically or verbally. It receives information internally through image-recognition, previously stored biological, gender, cultural, personal information. Stored information is what we call memory, or knowledge. Various parts of the brain receive information, process it, decide what to do about it, and send messages along neuronal circuits to other parts of the brain as thought or feeling, or to the body as behavior.

As LeDoux says, "Memory is a marvelous device...we can go back a moment, or most of a life. But as we all know, it's not perfect, and is certainly not literal. It's a reconstruction of facts and experiences on the basis of the way they were stored, *not as they actually occurred*. And it's a reconstruction by a brain that is different from the one that formed the memory....We are our memories, and without them, we are nothing." The self itself is nothing locatable or permanent, but only a temporary set of memories-as-self-image chosen in the moment by the brain to represent you. ('I' am cool, hip, good-looking, popular, a good writer, ballplayer—yeah, and sometimes not!) Nothing consistent, nothing permanent, you're one set of images one minute, another the next.

Does more memory or knowledge even make you smarter? Does memory or knowledge make for progress? Or does memory or knowledge/intellect get in the way of intelligence? Is there a difference between learning stored as knowledge and an ongoing state of open-minded learning?

Gene's Eye View

Pinker, with his genetic view of our brains ("the mind is an organ of computation engineered by natural selection"), says, "But if the mind has a complex innate structure, that does not mean that learning is unimportant...every part of human intelligence involves culture and learning....But learning is not a surrounding gas or force field, and it does not happen by magic. It is made possible by innate machinery designed to do the learning." We learn what we're wired to learn.

Gould says that the basic form of our human bodies and brains has not evidentially changed at all in the past 100,000 years. But in the past 10,000 years, "from the origin of agriculture to the Sears Building in Chicago, the entire panoply of human civilization—for better or for worse—has been built upon the capacities of an unaltered brain. Clearly, cultural change can vastly outstrip the maximal rate of natural Darwinian evolution." Education is our species' ability to rewire our circuits through learning and storing knowledge as memory, and to pass on that memorized learning from one generation to the next. It is education in this sense that has given us what endurance our species has and is a major factor in affecting our evolution.

Lest that educated endurance blow us up and wreck any sustainable environment for human beings, we had best understand just what it is we are teaching and learning and committing to memory storage in our brain's and body's neuronal circuitry.

Psychological Learning, Technological Learning

Krishnamurti, the philosopher in our own time who specifically addressed how our brains work, separates out psychological learning from technical learning. He says that life is not understood through a series of instructions. You can apply instructions to a dynamo, but life is not a machine—life can only be seen one moment at a time. "Intelligence comes when you are learning. In learning there is no end, and that is the beauty of life, the sacredness of life." (Bombay, Public Talk 2, 1958 from *The Complete Works of J. Krishnamurti*) He further says,

> *"We generally learn through study, through books through experience, or through being instructed. Those are the usual ways of learning. We commit to memory what to do and*

what not to do, what to think and what not to think, how to feel, how to react.

Now I think there is a totally different way of learning...which is not the accumulation of knowledge as memory....We accumulate various forms of knowledge—scientific, physiological, technological, and so on—and this knowledge is necessary for the physical well-being of man....The brain is an animalistic, progressive, evolutionary thing which...is everlastingly active in safeguarding and protecting itself—and in some measure it has to be; otherwise it would soon be destroyed.

Then what is learning? Is there a different kind of learning, a learning which is not cumulative, which doesn't become merely a background of memory...which doesn't cripple the mind but, on the contrary, gives it freedom? ...It is in the state of constant learning—not only from outward things, but also from inward things...constantly learning from everything without accumulation....Then your mind is always fresh; it looks at everything anew and not with the jaded look of knowledge." (Saanen, 1964, Public Talk 1)

Learning is the constant freedom to look, with no authority, not even the authority of your own memorized experience. Then you can see clearly how to act, how to live your life. Technical memory has its place, or you couldn't talk or remember your own name. But psychologically, living only according to memory means you aren't really living your life, you're just watching old movies. Technical memory must be at the service of, not dominate, intelligence.

Learning and Memory: Psychoneurophysiology

You yourself can best test the complexity and power of the small, crinkled organ inside your skull. Just sit still and close your eyes. Your imaginative ability, all those images based on all the sensory input you have memorized, will instantly create a whole new world inside your head. What's more, that world put together by your thoughts feels absolutely as real as the outside world.

This ability, this amazing power that we human beings have acquired during our evolution to perceive, combine, and memorize what happens outside us has made possible the skills and inventions, from washing machines to medicine to bombs, that make human life both more comfortable and more dangerous.

At the level of physics, nothing separates us from anything on earth or the heavens—all atoms together. Psychologically, however, this strange ability human brains possess to create an inner world makes us feel self-enclosed, cut off, lonely. To feel lonely is to feel afraid. To not understand this fear is to be dangerous.

For humans to go on enjoying the marvelous comforts and inventions of our brains and to avoid the psychological problems they cause, we must use the intelligence of our experience, not fear, to change the connections in our brains.

Always, it is experience that changes the brain. Change what you do, and you change the brain. Neuroscience uses the word plasticity to describe our human brain's capacity to change, and this ability to change makes it different from anything else we've yet discovered in our universe.

Restak describes it, "Plasticity is most evident during infancy. From a tiny ball of cells the brain first emerges, grows, and organizes itself. As the brain increases in size and complexity inside the womb, its growing cells interact with their environment and with one another. Newly formed neurons establish connections and those connections multiply.... Experience provides the basis for the formation of the connections and the transformation of those connections into circuits."

As LeDoux puts it, "Life is change, and the brain is a device for recording changes—for forming memories through learning. Learning and memory...fill in the details of who we are as we become a unique person."

But what is the nature of the neural changes that make up learning and memory? Learning is the changes in the activity of the synapses, the electrical/chemical firings between nerve cells; memory maintains these changes over time. To illustrate: if every time you skateboard down Elm Street, someone throws a rock at your head, you will soon stop skateboarding down Elm Street. Your body will tell your brain the rock hurts; your brain will learn from what your body tells it; the experience of the pain will be stored as memory; and you'll change your skateboarding route to Oak

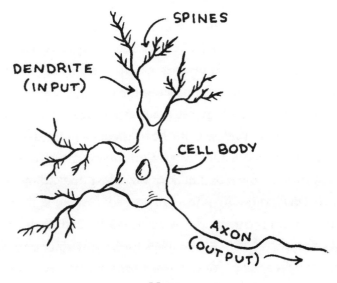

Neuron

Street instead. Life is a good teacher: it will tell you don't go this way, go that way. Our job is to listen up! It doesn't take a genius to hear what's good for us, what in the short or long run will kill us.

What Does Learning Look Like in the Brain?

All neurons have three basic parts: the cell body and two types of appendages. These two appendages are axons and dendrites. They are nerve fibers, and they act like telephone wires. Input enters the cell through the dendrites and outputs the message along axons. The nerve cells differs from other body cells because they have these nerve fibers. The cell body contains genetic material and also the ingredients, like proteins, to make short- and long-term memory, which are distinguished by their chemical requirements as well as their longevity. If animals, for instance, are given drugs that prevent the brain from making new proteins, they are able to learn normally but are unable to form long-lasting memories. Glutamate, calcium, enzymes called protein kinases to activate specific proteins, all have their tasks in the brain chemistry needed for learning, forming circuits, short- and long-term memories that make us what we are and make us do what we do.

Your brain is constantly firing. It is a hotbed of electrical and chemical activity. It's no use shrieking at other people if you don't like the product (your self) your brain is turning out. You'll need to reparent, reinstruct your own brain to make the alterations.

Ages and Stages of Development
Cause Different Reactions

Sabrina's family is having its weekly Friday night fight. Sabrina belongs to the popular crowd in her high school senior class; she knows that while this gives her a terrific endorphin buzz, that the price of popularity is having to keep ahead or get left behind and out. Sabrina is not just a clotheshorse, trend-setter, and party girl. She has plans for the next four years of college to major in political science. She plans law school for three more years after that. She wants to enter politics and eventually work in the West Wing of the White House, at the head and the heart of power.

Sabrina always wants to win the Friday night fight. The fights are not always about her on Friday nights, but Sabrina gets involved with all fights whatever and whoever the subject. Sabrina is as competitive with opinions as businesspeople with money or athletes on the field. She is never without a strongly held and defended opinion on anything. She needs to be right as if her life depended on it.

"I need to lead the march and the rally next Saturday," she says. "We're fighting for the right to vote on turning one of the town's golf courses into an inner city sports field and playground, buses and equipment included."

"Next Saturday is your grandmother's birthday, and we're having a celebration," her mother states firmly.

Sabrina takes a minute to marshal her arguments. She knows her grandmother feels her granddaughter's love enough not to care whether Sabrina misses a celebration for once. Half the time her grandmother, a writer busy with her own affairs, misses family occasions anyway.

"She'll get out of it somehow," shouts Sabrina's angry ten-year-old brother. "Sabrina always gets out of everything and I always get stuck with everything."

"Are you sure you want to involve yourself in this battle?" says her father. "You have exams coming up. And the battle you've picked this time is going to involve a lot more than picketing the garden club for their rose money to send to Bangladesh."

The baby propped up in her highchair near Sabrina's mother adds squeaks, squeals, and eventually howls to the family's verbal volleyball.

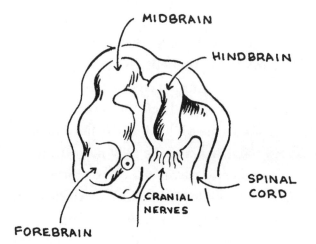

7 Weeks

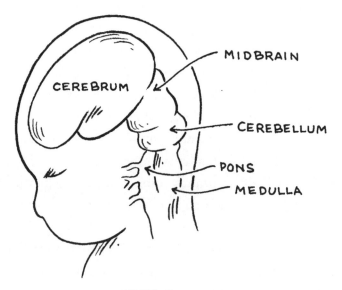

11 Weeks

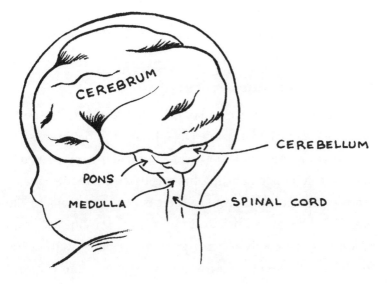

7 Months

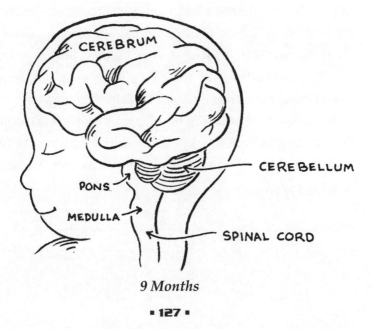

9 Months

Sabrina's and each family member's responses to the argument reflects their age and stage of development in their brains.

Development: Ages and Stages

Gestation: The uniform ball of cells that results from sperm penetrating egg contains the DNA blueprint that guides the construction of a whole body. The brain starts out as a crest of cells from which neurons, brain cells, begin to form major brain regions and migrate to their correct positions in the brain. Forebrain, midbrain, hindbrain form, but are soon hidden by the cerebral hemispheres, the outgrowth of the forebrain. At seven months into pregnancy, the cerebral hemispheres become 85% of the weight of the brain and wrinkle up and fold in on themselves to fit into the space. The cerebral cortex, the outer 2 millimeters of the hemispheres (cortex means rind in Latin) contains two-thirds of the brain's 100 billion neurons and about three-quarters of the 100 trillion interneuronal connections. At birth, a human baby brain already has its 100 billion neurons, and its cortex is ten times larger than an adult macaque monkey's.

Neurons in the newborn have formed only a few connections among themselves, but they multiply during the first year into thickets of receptive dendrites and message-sending axons.

Childhood: During childhood, the brain contains a lot more neurons than it needs, and pruning away begins, forming personality and skills. Unused pathways disappear, repeatedly used connections are reinforced. Young children learn and increase their capacities for attention and memory, acquiring skills to master their universes. Equally, their growth can be stunted. Romanian orphanages became infamous because the children housed in them remained untouched, rarely spoken to, unstimulated. Parents adopting them found their brains had not developed bonding and relationship skills, language skills, and they lacked both curiosity and the ability to control fear, rage, and many of their behaviors.

Adolescence: The pruning process is pretty well accomplished in most areas of the brain with the great exception we have noted: the prefrontal cortex. Most adolescent problems are due to immaturity in this area (judgement problems, impulsiveness, constant mood swings, and the tug of war between needing someone to be in charge and rebellion toward greater independence).

Adulthood: The adult brain is booted up and functioning in all its areas if all has gone well. Its general health will depend on not just what has been programmed in, but its ability to pay intelligent attention to what is actually, currently going on inside and outside its own brain. Again it should be remembered, in the words of Alcoholics Anonymous founder Bill Wilson, that "most of us are to some extent emotionally ill and frequently wrong."

Old Age: We now know that the brains of older people, unless there is disease, stroke, or dementia, retain plasticity and can go on changing and functioning. The body degenerates; the brain need not as long as people continue to use it. Older people can neglect their brain power or use it into their 80s, 90s, as long as they live. Second childhood is a choice older people sometimes make, not a necessity, unless diseased.

Back to Sabrina and the Friday Night Family Fight

Sabrina at seventeen is still a work in progress. Her life, body, and brain are at their most flexible, with everything—personality, moods, emotions, plans for the future, thoughts—constantly in flux. Her frontal lobes are being pruned as new life skills are learned. Her hormones, her neurochemistry, her neuron connections are changing, with her emotional or limbic system in overdrive and her prefrontal lobes, the seat of judgement and impulse control, not yet entirely mature. But pruning continues as she learns the life skills she needs to do what she wants to do: be popular, negotiate with people well enough to be out in front of the pack and be a leader in directions she thinks best. Her brain is already honing itself in diplomatic, politically able thinking and behavior, at school, in the community, among her family.

Sabrina's brother, at ten, has less control. He has an overabundance of unpruned neurons constantly growing new connections, and with still immature prefrontal lobes, little self-control. He is almost entirely at the mercy of his limbic system and the impulses of his prepubescent growing body. He overreacts to everything and is still very much the center of his own universe, not necessarily out of purposeful selfishness but a lack of ability to form appropriate judgements of needs beyond his own.

Sabrina's parents have their own problems: at their age, they are sandwiched between the needs of two generations as well as attending to their own lives and work. Hopefully they are aware (many people are not) that new connections form in the brain throughout their life spans, that their own brains remain flexible and adaptable, that they can change their behavior and their rules even when it's hard to alter their own conditioning. If they can keep this in mind, they will be able to balance their responses to their children and judge properly the various family needs, including their own.

As for Sabrina's grandmother, because she has continued to exercise all her faculties her thinking has remained intact and vigorous. Her attitude is, "Everyone begins aging in their twenties. I haven't finished yet." Her two kinds of memory, short-term and long-term, function well enough, she says, and when there's a memory problem she thinks it has to do with no longer paying attention to what doesn't interest her, whether in the present (short-term, working memory in the prefrontal cortex of a new telephone number) or in the past (long-term storage which involves protein synthesis and various regions of the brain including the cerebellum and motor cortex, the hippocampus, the medial temporal lobe, the amygdala). The frontal lobe is involved in transferring short-term, working-memory to long-term memory, and she says she does less of that than ever. "If I want to know whether Columbus discovered America in 1491 or 1492, I can look it up in a book. If I want to know how old Sabrina is now, I can ask her."

As for the six-month-old baby, although its brain is busy wiring itself and forming its brain circuits well enough to babble and chew, look for, grab, play with a toy, recognize and smile at family faces, sit up and hold its head steady in a highchair, without language skills it can't make any contribution to Sabrina's Friday night problems other than to interrupt with squeaks and burbles of satisfaction or yowls to get its own needs attended to. Six more months, and language and a more developed emotional life will begin.

About You and Your Family

Try to pay objective attention the next time your family argues and try to figure out what their brains are doing according to age, stage, personality, biological, historical, neuropsychological profile. Understanding them might get you farther than shrieking at them.

CHAPTER NINE

Evolutionary Psychology:
Evolution And Your Brain
How Mental and Behavior Patterns Evolve—
Use It or Lose It—The Developing Self

Jocks and Nerds

We never stop talking to ourselves. We never stop seeing pictures, hearing sound tracks, running snatches of dialogue in our brains. All this inside dreamworld, sometimes tapes of romance and glory, often a horror show, not only prevents us from seeing what is actually going on in the world but makes us crazy, high, angry, or scared. Why our brains do this is because image-making was our species' major survival skill in the first place. And despite our technical advances, we have not changed psychologically in the four or more million years of developing humanity. We still don't really distinguish between dangerous groups of atoms like a rabid tiger from a new kid in school—if it's a not-me, we're suspicious. Even with plenty of space and food on our planet, we're still killing and competing instead of cooperating: can we change this human brain, this neurobiology? or are we doomed to kill each other off?

I keep remembering Pinker's remark: "Human evolution is the original revenge of the nerds."

No matter how hard football coaches, soccer moms, and ice hockey dads try, they can't turn human bodies into much. Compared to other animals, we have no great physical strength or speed, we have comparatively slow physical reflexes, no useful tails, sensitive noses or trunks, poisonous fangs, flight feathers.

We do have upright posture, frontal vision, and thumbs that give us precision manipulation. But as Pinker says, essentially it is not our bodies but our brains, "our behavior and the mental programs that organize it" that allow us "humans control of the fate of tigers, rather than vice versa."

So the brains of this Earth, not the jocks, are in charge. We need to understand, therefore, not only the evolution of our biological agenda, but especially the intellect in our species, the modern mind in particular. It is at once our greatest asset, and our most dangerous.

What Is Evolution?

Evolve, from the Latin *evolvere*, simply means to unroll, unfold, change.

Astrophysicists like Stephen Hawking tell us that our cosmic history goes back fifteen billion years when a tight, dense ball containing all matter in the universe exploded in a big bang and flung its matter outward. If fifteen billion years of cosmic history is represented by one year, then our whole history occurs in the last ten hours. As evolutionary biologist Carl Sagan says in his *Dragons of Eden*, a timeline of human history spans just a few hours in the universe's fifteen billion years—from December 31 to the first second of New Year's Day—and this includes the time from the appearance of the first ancestor of apes and humans to human beings, their spread from Africa over the Earth, their first civilizations, their art, their language and writing, their invention of science and technology.

Again, evolution just means change, not necessarily progress or even improvement. Clearly, what evolution is not is a ladder, with us at some glorious pinnacle. We have believed this, as Gould suggests, the same way we believed the Earth was flat, or that it was the center of the universe— and our arrogance is in for another rude awakening if we don't see we are just another scrap of life tumbling about this planet. What evolution is not, is either predictable or directional, says Dr. Stephen Jay Gould in his book *Full House*. Simply put, as environment changes due to planetary or cosmic events, organisms change and adopt. We mustn't forget we are only a tiny scrap of life, sprouted just yesterday on the larger scale of time. "We grasp at the straw of progress…crave progress as our best hope for retaining human arrogance in an evolutionary world." Gould likes to quote Freud saying that all major revolutions in the history of science…end in the dethronement of human arrogance. When our more sophisticated equipment identified our Earth as a tiny satellite of an ordinary star at the edge of a small galaxy amid a cluster of galaxies among many such galactic clusters in the universe, we really had to wonder: 1) just how important humans are in the whole scheme of things, and 2) whether we have any more importance at all than anything else in the universe.

It's a constant shock, even to the individual's system, to discover and rediscover daily that each of us is not the center of the universe.

Zoltan Torey, in his *Crucible of Consciousness*, suggests a further, interesting possibility for human responsibility: that we are what matter has generated out of itself, and that a "mind-boosted brain" (the ability to decode and reprogram itself intelligently) might make us the consciousness of the universe, but only if we learn what he calls biospheric morality. Clearly, we have a lot of work to do on our neurobiological brain-generated selves first before humans qualify for the consciousness of the universe. We might, for instance, like to graduate from "human" to "humane," as Buddha, Jesus, Krishnamurti, and other perennial philosophers and many scientists suggest. See *Who Said What? Philosophy Quotes for Teens* in this teen book series.

Origin of Us Big-Brain Apes

Charles Darwin, in his *Origin of Species*, suggested the now provable fact that we are descended from the same primate as all the other great apes with whom we still share 97%-99% of our genetic material—cousins all, descended during a time span between 7 million and 40,000 years ago from a mouse-sized creature that lived in trees on insects and fruit.

It was the bigger brain in relation to body size that made us different from the other big apes, and within that brain, some major differences in neurological circuitry. The wired-in ability for speech-language-learning and therefore communication with each other, and along with this the ability to pass on information to our children so they didn't have to reinvent the wheel each generation but could build on past technology—this was a major different capacity from other apes. *Symbolic thought* that led to the making of tools, the use of fire, the creation of art and writing increased the busy nervous activity of our brains and made for increasingly complex circuitry. From the size and shape of skulls found together with the nearby tools, artifacts, and art once produced by the brains inside those skulls, primatologists can put together much of our neurological history.

Professor Daniel Dennett discusses, in his *Consciousness Explained*, three processes in the evolution of human consciousness:

1. Life wants to reproduce itself: to reproduce, it has to stay alive; to stay alive, it needs to tell the difference between me and not-me. Even molecules in your immune system are shape-detectors so they can fight disease.

2. To stay alive, any organism, our brains included, must produce "future." A clam grows a shell and hopes for the best. Human brains build better neighborhoods and bigger rock piles. We anticipate.

3. Good Tricks—"our ancestors learned some Good Tricks with their adjustable hardware"—language, cooking, agriculture. These are passed on through imitation/teaching/learning, but are being encoded into our genome by natural selection. Mother Nature may be blind, but we tend to marry and reproduce more babies with mates who are the healthiest, most adaptable, cleverest at staying alive and ahead.

A Strange Species with a Really Good Trick

Dennett describes, in his *Consciousness Explained*, "a species of primate in South America, more gregarious than most other mammals, with a curious behavior. The members of the species often gather in groups, large and small, and in the course of their mutual chattering...they are induced to engage in bouts of involuntary, convulsive respiration, a sort of loud, helpless, mutually reinforcing group panting that sometimes is so severe as to incapacitate them...these attacks seem to be sought out by most members of the species, some of whom even appear to be addicted to them...

"...the species is Homo sapiens [which does indeed inhabit South America, among other places], and the behavior is laughter."

Is this hooting and panting and frenzy an advance of some kind? If so, why?

The Origin of Species

In the *Origin of Species*, Darwin describes evolution:

1. All organisms tend to produce more offspring than can possibly survive.

2. Offspring vary among themselves, and are not carbon copies of an immutable or unchanging type.

3. At least some of this variation is passed down by inheritance to future generations. (See heredity scientist Gregor Mendel's later principles of inheritance and current genomics.)

4. If many offspring must die (for not all can be accommodated in nature's limited ecology)...survivors will tend to be those individuals with variations that are fortuitously best suited to *changing local environments*. The genomic blueprint ensures that the offspring of these survivors will resemble their successful parents. The sum of these best survival traits through time will produce evolutionary change. Darwin called this process natural selection. Another word for new trait is mutation.

Natural selection is about "adaptation to changing local environments," not progress, and adaptive heredity may even lead to simplification, not complexity. Or even just a change in color. An example of adaptation, and therefore survival, are the white moths of Great Britain turning black to match the soot as Britain industrialized. Neuroscientists continue to argue about whether the changes are limited to only physical changes or, in the case of some species like our own, include cultural evolutionary changes as well. This is where Gould's argument for biological potential, not just biological determinism, allows all of us to change course.

A Teenager Named Lucy: the Brain-Body Connection

Lucy was a teenage girl who lived about 3.5 million years ago in Kenya. She changed her behavior, rewired her brain circuits in several important regions. Because Lucy was our common human ancestor, her rewired brain was passed down through all our generations. Among other traits, this teenage girl changed the sex lives of the human race forever. Several evolutionary biologists support this theory. Lucy, technically an early young hominid we call Australopithecus afarensis, came out of the East African jungle onto the grasslands. Although her jaw was more forward and her forehead still sloped, her brain was already big for her body size: Lucy was a human teenage girl, and a teenage mom as well.

Lucy was looking for food. The jungles were shrinking in the drying climate, and she came out onto the savanna to forage. She was carrying her baby, and to protect her child she rose and remained on two legs so she could keep watch for predators over the savanna grasses. To opposable thumbs and frontal vision, she now added two more distinguishing features of the human race and so altered our neuronal circuitry forever. To search for food, and to protect her baby, she altered the position of her hips and fixed the human spine in an upright position. Even more startling, she used her eyes and brain to create and retain images. She could not fight predators larger than she. *But she could form an image, remember, and retreat for cover while the predator was still distant.*

Memory and Image Making

Memory and image-making are both necessary for passing on culture and technology as well as individual resentment and global war, but the point remains: it was an African teenage girl's hip that changed our species, our brains and so-cial habits, forever. *In her new standing up position, Lucy now looked her boyfriend, her mate, in the eye, inventing not only fron-tal sex but human sexual relationships.* As Paul Jordan suggests in his *Early Man*, bipedalism changed our sexual habits. We no longer necessarily made love like most other animals. Instead, we looked each other in the eye. We recognized spirit and psyche in each other as well as body, thus changing the nature of sexual attractions, bonded mating, family, social relationships. Jordan adds, "The big penises and full breasts of the human line may have evolved in step with bipedal-ism, changing the nature of sexual attractions...and encouraging even more mental agility to negotiate the so-cial scene...at all events, bipedalism marks the turning point at which homonids and pongids, human beings and human-like apes, decisively parted company." Of course, Lucy did not accomplish all this all by herself. But it was Lucy's kind, whose remains are found in Tanzania and Ethiopia, to whom we owe our upright posture, who freed our hands for tools, and who changed our relationships.

That the brain and body function as a connected, physi-cal unit each influencing the other, is seen in the brain's cells, chemicals, tissues, the number of cortical areas, interconnec-tions, their hookup to motor and decision regions of the frontal lobes. As Pinker states, "The human brain, too, tells an evolutionary story...the primate brain must have been considerably re-engineered to end up as a human brain...major lobes and patches of the brain have been revamped…olfactory bulbs…shriveled…the main cortical areas for vision and movement have shrunk…the primary visual cortex smaller, later areas for complex-form processing expand, as do the tempero-parietal areas that shunt visual information to the language and conceptual regions. The areas for hearing, especially for understanding speech, have grown, and the prefrontal lobes, the seat of deliberate thought and planning, have ballooned to twice what a primate our size should have."

But what Pinker goes on to add is that there could be even greater differences, only "virtually nothing is known about the functioning microcircuitry of the human brain, because there is a shortage of volunteers willing to give up their brains to science before they are dead." We still do not know how or when our lineage developed symbolic thought, how the modern human brain converts chemistry and nerve connections in the brain into consciousness. We don't understand consciousness any more than we understand biogenesis, the origin of life and why, four billion years ago, some inert chemicals suddenly grew "ert," alive. Those of you who have read the previous book in this science series for teens, *In and Out of Your Mind: Teen Science, Human Bites*, will remember to avoid crackpot theories about what we don't actually know. There is a lot we don't, can't, or can't yet know, either because the human brain is limited, or because our current use of the human brain is limited.

HUMAN NATURE: HOW WE GOT THIS WAY

Up on Our Feet

Three and a half million years ago, Lucy's and her friends' bipedalism freed their hands for more complex tool-making, hunting, shelter-building, fire-making and cooking— and all this activity increased the mental complexities of their brains which in turn increased their physical and technological skills.

Their increased skills and mental curiosity, and especially their search for food, led their descendants, just a few thousand people back then, to spread out from Africa all over the rest of the world about three million years later, 50,000 or so years ago. But it is well to remember in our sometimes color, class, caste, teenager-phobic world that the first ancestors, the first human people, the first scientists, artists, kings, emperors, civilizations, were not middle-aged, middle-class white, yellow, or pink people. They were brainy, inventive, courageous black teenagers—from whom everyone, every human family, has sprung.

Times and Appearances

35-31 million years ago: Monkey-like creatures.

23 mya: Hominoid primates, the superfamily to which we and the great apes belong—gibbons, orangutans, gorillas, and chimpanzees and bonobos.

6-7 mya: We diverge from chimpanzees.

4.4 mya: Ardipithecus ramidus: in Ethiopia, the earliest hominid biped, apelike but upright.

4.2 mya: Australopithecus anamensis: in Kenya, definitely crossed line from ape to human.

3.8-3.0 mya: Australopithecus afarensis, in Ethiopia and Tanzania—Lucy is the most famous.

3.0-2.0 mya: Australopithecus africanus, South Africa—until 2 mya.

2.0-1.4 mya: The robusts, Paranthropus boisei, P. robustus, and others were among the early people living in Africa.

2.5-1.8 mya: Fossils announce the earliest period of the genus Homo, among them Homo habilis (our early tool man or handywoman) and Homo ergaster, the first modern body form. Hominids of some kind had reached China and Java by about 1.8 mya.

1 mya: By 1 mya, Homo erectus may have reached the Far East, and became well established in Java and in China— Peking Man— with bigger brains, smaller teeth, perhaps language use and conceptual thought.

600,000-200,000 years ago: Homo heidelbergensis—Africa, Europe, China. This is probably more than one species, a group of hominid types best known for Homo neanderthalensis who inhabited Europe, Western Asia, and Africa. Fire was used, about 400,000 ya, along with the improvement of structural features of caves and other shelters.

200,000-30,000 ya: Neanderthal people may have coexisted with us from Europe to Asia. They used tools and language, buried their dead, supported their old and sick. They are a divergent line of hominids from us Homo sapiens, not our ancestors. There is, so far, no evidence of intermarriage.

150,000-100,000 ya: Homo sapiens fossil remains found in Africa. Homo ergaster seems to have been the first modern human form, and also the first, 50,000 years ago, to spread out over the world from Africa. They went south to Australia, then north through the Middle East to Central Asia. And 40,000 years ago, human beings spread out from Central Asia, west to Europe, and east to China.

In European sites, human remains are only about 40,000 years old. Fossils tell us we had stone-working technology, art like the great cave paintings, musical wind instruments, sewn clothes and personal adornments—clearly these people were us. By 20,000 years ago, we had crossed Russia, the Bering Straits, and arrived in the Americas. We stayed in the north to become Inuits, and headed south to become tribes from the Sioux to the Aztecs.

We are getting crowded on our Earth. Where do we go next?

CHAPTER TEN

Sociobiology, Social Psychology
How and Why Your Family, Group, Society Behave—
Why Is Homo Sapiens, Like Nature in General,
Such a Seemingly Nasty Business?

Simple: the Group Behaves the
Same Way Each One of Us Behaves:
We Just Don't Like It When They Do

And we have names to describe the sciences dealing with everyone's behavior: social psychology, sociobiology, psychosocial dynamics, evolutionary psychosociology, political science, and, of course, cultural cognitive science and neuroscience. There are ethologists, ethnologists, geneticists, evolutionists, anthropologists, sexologists, zoologists, psychiatrists, sociologists, physiologists, neurochemists, physicists, metaphysicists, ethicists, the artificial intelligence, computer/electronics/robotics, and cyborg crowd—even astrologists and feng shui practitioners. I may have missed some, but you get the point. Everybody has an explanation for why we behave the way we do, and suggestions for what we can do about it.

The Psychology of Social Relations

There is no mysterious answer to why groups behave the way they do, from parents and children, between siblings, to boyfriends and girlfriends, cliques and crowds, towns, cities, whole nations, religions, and cultures.

The group behaves the way your own brain behaves; the family, the country, the whole world is just you, me, multiplied by over six billion. As Steven Pinker says, "Inborn motives...put us into conflict with one another. Given that our brains were shaped by natural selection, it could hardly be otherwise. Natural selection is driven by the competition among genes to be represented in the next generation....Everyone alive today is a descendant of millions of generations of...having winners as ancestors."

This doesn't mean, Pinker goes on to say, that we all hide murder, theft, and rape in our hearts. Natural selection provides humans with mental programs that "assess the opportunities and risks at hand and either compete or cooperate accordingly." Pinker's genetic view of evolution: "the mind is an organ of computation engineered by natural selection," and our social motives are equally a matter of survival of the fittest. Each of our brains has programmed circuitry for "kin and non-kin, and about parents, children, siblings, dates, spouses, acquaintances, friends, rivals, allies, and enemies."

Religions and folk music can talk or sing all they want about loving the whole world. We don't. Our genes are selfish, they want to survive, which means competition. Children want what their parents have, siblings want what the other siblings have, from parental preference to property. Families want what other families have, countries what other countries possess. This does not mean we are purposely bloodthirsty, vicious killers of other species, or rapists of land and sea. It means that genes are thoughtless, selfish, oriented to survival.

It also means that because part of our genetic inheritance is to understand why we do what we do, we can alter what we do and remember what Stephen Jay Gould says in *The Mismeasure of Man*: "Human uniqueness lies in the flexibility of what our brain can do. What is intelligence, if not the ability to face problems in an unprogrammed manner? If intelligence sets us apart…I think it probable that natural selection acted to maximize the flexibility of our behavior. What would be more adaptive for a learning, thinking animal: genes selected for aggression, spite, and xenophobia; or selection for learning rules that can generate aggression in appropriate circumstances and peacefulness in others?"

Family Neuronal Psychology

Preference, especially among social animals like humans, is given to family to keep the family gene pool alive. Parentage and family ties and obligational behaviors are programmed in, like behavior among those cute meerkats of South Africa, and this occasions a greater degree of sympathy and trust for kin than for non-kin. Blood really is thicker than water," says Pinker, and "no aspect of human existence is untouched by that part of our psychology. Families are important in all societies, and their core is a mother and her biological children. All societies have marriage." When police statistics refer to high homicide rates among relatives, only 2%-6% are done in by blood relatives, the rest are spouses, in-laws, and step-relations.

Marriage: Its Neuronal Psychology

The psychobiology of marriage, or why married people usually don't kill each other despite their being from different past families, is the fact that the future survival of their genes is based in their shared children. For the same reason, extended families—grandparents, aunts and uncles, and cousins—who share genetic interests tend to cooperate to protect family interests and shared loyalties. Until recently, romantic love was considered silly for survival reasons: women and children were property to be used to consolidate family interests.

SOCIOBIOLOGY, SOCIAL PSYCHOLOGY

Genetic Psychobiology of Family, Countries, Organized Religions

No matter how politicians and television evangelists try to win popularity by standing for family values, profoundly "every political and religious movement in history has sought to undermine the family," says journalist Ferdinand Mount. Clearly, of course, the family is a "rival coalition competing for a person's loyalties." Equally clearly, successful states and religions have ways to make country and church extensions of family interests.

Parent-Child and Sibling Genetic Behavior

Evolutionarily speaking, nature, including human nature, may be pretty, but it is also nasty, violent, self-centered. Genetically, though, parents are the least selfish of organisms, and after them, siblings. Bird and mammal parents, in order to leave the descendants which is the goal and reason for being alive, bequeath fifty percent of their genes, share calories, invest time, often risk their lives for their offspring. Human parents are resented because they never give everything their offspring want from them, though we should understand we are lucky to belong to a species that gives anything at all. Human siblings are resented for taking a share of parental attention and resources, when we ought to be grateful our older or stronger family members don't kill us outright, as siblings do in other species to get all the resources for themselves.

Parent-Child Neuronal Conflict

We may get our food and shelter from our parents, but we get much of our neuronal information from our peers. Our socialization, our personalities which are the sum of our survival adaptations, many scientists now think are not just due to our parent/family genes and environment, but are the result of children's and teenagers' peer group culture. As children grow older, they have to figure out not only how to survive in their families, but in their peer group culture. As their peers will in future be the group with whom they compete and cooperate for survival, as well as their source of information and opportunity, it is thought by many social psychologists that our neuronal circuitry drives and is driven as much by peer culture as family genetic culture and is at the base of parent/child conflict.

What is clear is that as we are, so the world is. As our brains behave, the world behaves and then returns in a loop to shape our brains and behavior. But it begins and ends with each one of us. Anyone still looking to shriek out the blame needs to be placed firmly in front of a mirror.

It's 'All in the Family'—Our Genes Tell Us Everyone Alive Is Related

Every single human being on the planet Earth is literally, provably, your relative. This absolute fact has been recently proved yet again by Dr. Spencer Wells, a 31-year-old population geneticist who traveled, with a portable laboratory, to test the genetic material in drops of blood taken from local populations around the world, and to trace the exact routes our ancestors traveled when they left Africa. We know our ancestors' routes from cultural and fossil remains dated by archaeologists and anthropologists. We know that these people were our ancestors and that we are descended from them because of population geneticists like Wells, who runs his own Human Genetics Department at Oxford University.

In his *Journey of Man*, a National Geographic special aired in December 2002, Wells began in Africa where all of us began, among Lucy's descendants. He started with the small, surviving tribe of Song Bushman who had stayed put in Africa, and who, among other retained characteristics of early humans, still speak in clicks as we all once probably did. Their skin is a medium hue and could go darker or lighter depending on whether the natural sun-block in all our skins, melanin, was necessary for the climate or not. Their features are neither narrow-nosed nor especially broad, their eyes neither exactly Caucasian nor Mongolian, they are neither the shortest nor tallest people. And they are still there, for a scientist to draw blood and examine their DNA on the spot. Wells did exactly this!

He then followed the fossil/artifacts trail of the African exodus as the Ice Age African drought, killing off our prey animals, pushed us to look north for food. It seems there were only a very few of us who were the first travelers, one hundred and fifty humans or so from whom the rest of us in the rest of the world are descended. We left Africa about

50,000 years ago, went north through the Middle East to Central Asia, where some went West to Europe 40,000 years ago, some East to China, some through Southeastern Asia down through Indonesia to settle in Australia where the blood DNA markers of Aborigines today prove their descent from African arrivals 40,000 years ago. Wells proved also, through DNA markers extrapolated from drops of blood in his portable lab, that Mongols from Central Asia migrated through Siberia, a few snow-hungry reindeer herders crossed—perhaps only twenty or thirty of us—the Bering Straits to become, about 15,000 years ago, the Inuits, the Navajo, the Incas, and all the other American tribes. Mostly the search for food pushed us on, but curiosity and territorial aggression also.

Wells, interested in the 10,000-year-gap between the 50,000 years ago when we left Africa and the 40,000 years that date our fossil/artifacts remains in Europe, discovered the reason. From the DNA markers in the Y chromosome which he used as a constant, he discovered that humans did not go directly through the Middle East north to Europe, but that all of us first went up to Central Asia, the grassy steppes of Kazakhstan. Kazakhstan was open and full of good hunting animals like the savannas they had left behind in Africa. Kazakhstan—think of the great horsepeople, the Cossaks, who came from there, Silk Road caravans, the Mongol herds and hordes roaming what is still a huge space on any map. This is where the ancestors of Eastern and Western peoples lived, and continue to live. Their features, too, contain all the marks of all the world's people, Eastern/Western eyes, coloring, noses, just as their blood drops carry the DNA material that, like a time machine, tells us everyone alive today is related.

The Bushmen of Africa's Kalahari Desert still click. But their genetic material tells every one of us who would like to offer Spencer Wells a drop of blood that we are all relatives, we were all originally African, we were all originally black.

As Bayard Rustin, friend of Dr. Martin Luther King, Jr. and organizer of the 1963 Civil Rights March on Washington said, "We are all one. And if we don't know it, we will learn it the hard way."

Science and Religion/Philosophy

Daniel Dennett says in his new book *Freedom Evolves* that, "culture, morality, and freedom are as much a result of evolution by natural selection as our physical and genetic attributes." Yet, he adds, "genetic determinism does not imply inevitability." He says all great philosophers and religious thinkers were involved with the science of their day, their quest for scientific knowledge. "Just look at Aristotle, or Hume, or Kant, or Mill, or William James….The vision of philosophy as somehow isolated from the sciences…is not to be honored."

Albert Einstein, who laid the groundwork for the twentieth century's two fundamental theories, general relativity and quantum theory, said, "I want to know how God created this world."

The great theoretical physicist and Einstein's successor, Stephen Hawking, sought not only science's holy grail, the Theory of Everything, but what Hawking calls "the mind of God."

Two points are clear to all great thinkers in fields of both science and religion:

1. Not only are we all related, but give or take a talent or personality quirk, in any language, *we all have the same brain.*

2. The origin of life is a mystery we haven't yet solved, but its conditions, life's cruelty and suffering, we can do something about because *changing our attitudes and our behavior will change the wiring in our suffering brains.*

What You Are, the World Is

"What is the relationship between yourself and the misery, the confusion, in and around you? Surely this confusion, this misery, did not come into being by itself. You and I have created it, not a capitalist nor a communist nor a fascist society, but you and I have created it in our relationship with each other. What you are within has been projected without, onto the world; what you are, what you think and what you feel, what you do in your everyday existence, is projected outwardly, and that constitutes the world. If we are

miserable, confused, chaotic within, by projection that becomes the world, that becomes society, because the relationship between yourself and myself, between myself and another is society—society is the product of our relationship—and if our relationship is confused, egocentric, narrow, limited, national, we project that and bring chaos into the world.

What you are, the world is. So your problem is the world's problem. Surely, this is a simple and basic fact, is it not? In our relationship with the one or the many we seem somehow to overlook this point all the time. We want to bring about alteration through a system or through a revolution in ideas or values based on a system, forgetting that it is you and I who create society, who bring about confusion or order by the way in which we live. So we must begin near, that is, we must concern ourselves with our daily existence, with our daily thoughts and feelings and actions which are revealed in the manner of earning our livelihood and in our relationship with ideas or beliefs."

— J. Krishnamurti, *What Are You Doing with Your Life?*

"Nature helped us to evolve physically. We must cooperate with nature to evolve psycologically by mutating, transforming our minds."

— Kishore Khairnar

CHAPTER ELEVEN

Neuroscience: Our Adaptable Brains

Intelligence—Consciousness, Artificial Intelligence, Cyborgs, Robots, and You—We Can Make Conscious Intellects, Not Intelligence

Computational Theory of Our Brains

The brain, according to neuroscientists like Pinker, is a soft-tissue computer, an evolution-determined information processor, and its fundamental activity is exactly that: information processing. He reminds us that human cognition is the reception, transmission, and processing of information in the human brain. When our senses receive information, our brains match that information against vast libraries of already stored images. As we know, this happens along our brain's axons (output fibers) and dendrites (input fibers)— one nerve cell sends an electrical signal across a synapse (space), where it changes to a chemical one and is received as information by the next nerve cell.

A density of atoms, a configuration of light waves and sound waves, are perceived, and the brain matches it all up into red/feathers/beak/crest/bird, and then further matches this to the image and words—male cardinal.

Another density of atoms, a configuration of light waves and sound waves, comes along, and the brain matches all that up to a previously stored image of my boyfriend Sam or my girlfriend Shannon—or my mother yelling at me to stop jumping my skateboard and wash my hands for dinner.

We do not, cannot, know what is out there. All we can know about the world are the images our brains have created and stored.

And our complex brains have stored trillions and trillions of interconnected and multifaceted images, ideas, representations both singly and in layers and layers of combinations. We have an inexhaustible supply, as Pinker says, of mental representations. He suggests that when Plato described the prisoners in the cave who only saw shadows on the cave wall of the real world outside, he was describing the skull as our cave, and our images as the shadows. If all this seems a stretch, remember your physics: everything is atoms and molecules—it is we who turn it all into kangaroos and daisies.

All this activity can be tracked, from the hippocampus and connected systems storing long-term memories to the short-term circuitry of the frontal lobes. The human brain is a highly flexible, subtle, coded process of mental computation.

Artificial Intellects: Computers and Robots that Outperform Our Own

So many computers do our work, we are almost not aware of them all anymore. What's more, they do it faster and more accurately than we can. You can buy an artificial brain cheaper than an artificial leg, and it will calculate, store, and retrieve facts, print a book, play chess, talk and sing to you. You can buy software, programs that will balance your money, pay your bills, find you prescription drugs, fit the right size jeans to your bottom, diagnose your diseases and your cars. There are robots and robotic arms in factories, in research labs, in surgeries. There are tiny artificial intelligence programs under most car hoods these days, and in this electronic-gadget country, in desk and hand-held personal computers, games, and toys for all ages. We may not have personalized robotic boyfriends or girlfriends, parents, teachers, sports coaches, beauty-makeover stylists, or personal assistants to make your bed, pick last year's junk out from your garage, or imitate you so you can hitch out of town for the weekend—but how far off is any of this?

How About a Cyborg—a Human Being Linked to and Dependent on a Mechanical Device?

The implications of brains melding with machines is another scientific two-edged sword like splitting the atom. Energy, or bombs? A cure for paralysis, or a race of monsters? "Brains and electronics can communicate because they have a common language: electricity," states Nell Boyce in a 2002 *U.S. News & World Report* article on cyborgs and electronic brain implants.

The medical implications are stupendous. Four years ago, neurologist Philip Kennedy announced a system that enabled a man, paralyzed and speechless after a stroke, to move a computer cursor simply by thinking about it. Two electrodes were implanted in a region of his brain associated with hand movement, and after two months of practice the brain figured out how to generate electrical signals that would move the cursor to spell out words. More common implants act as pacemakers for the brain, sending electrical impulses to restore order in disordered brains. Fifteen thousand people with Parkinson's disease have electronic chest implants now sending signals to electrodes deep in their brains. Medical scientists expect to be able to treat depression and obsessive-compulsive disorders with implanted electrodes that detect abnormal activity. Implanted neurochips and microelectrodes may permit computer-controlled arm and leg movements in people who have lost the use of their limbs.

Naturally, the military got right in there with an interest in using mind control for warfare. Joseph Fins, a medical ethicist at Cornell University says, "historical legacy is a scary one...brain implants can help people, if the devices allow patients to have control, not be under control." And then there's the possible problem of creating a superior caste of people, with a superior caste of cyborgs—people who have money spending it on brain implants, microchips, to enhance intellect or memory, and therefore position and power. We may one day have chips to treat Alzheimer's and other mind-destroying diseases, but we have to be careful of the 'cyberpunks' who want to 'jack in' to their computers, to 'upgrade' their brains as it were, or 'email' thoughts to or control other cyborgs. The new nanotechnology, promising molecule-sized robots, has been novelized by Michael Crichton in his new techno-thriller *Prey*. Supersmall nanobots the size of molecules could eventually yield medical miracles like bacteria-size disease fighters. But the weapons' potential of tiny, body-invading particles has not, as you can imagine, been ignored by the war-makers among us. *You could be used as a bomb.*

The combination of brains, bodies, and silicon, like all technological innovation, needs ethical monitoring so we don't slide by degrees from science into nightmare. It is so necessary for teenagers to understand what is going on in science and technology, at least in general terms, for this reason: informed, you can see what you are being handed by natural history, science, cultural attitudes. It's is up to you what you do with it, provided you make up your own mind and don't just take in what is handed to you, take in, like a computer, a robot or a cyborg, whatever has been discovered, programmed, or implanted.

We Can Create Information-Processing Intellects: but Where Does Intelligence Come From?

Like the origin of life, the origin of intelligence is still unknown. We can find no part of the physical brain where intelligence receptors seem to reside. Our technology permits us to see scans of brain areas where intellection—thought, information-processing—and the brain's other capabilities such as vision or hearing or language, the deliberate judgement and planning of the frontal lobes, the busy activity of the amygdala and limbic systems of our emotional circuitry take place. We can literally watch our brains think and feel. We can watch our intellects function.

What we cannot see is the functioning of intelligence, another word for insight, mind, awareness. This intelligence functions, oddly, only when the intellect, when thought which is based on memory and the past, shuts up so that something new can come into being. It is in the gaps between thoughts that intelligence or mind functions, and it is found on no x-ray, PET scan, or MRI. Nor can it be programmed into any computer, bot, or borg.

For the sake of clarity, just so we can communicate, we'll define intellect, intelligence, and cognition this way for now:

intelligence: mind, awareness, insight, understanding, perception in the moment—the something *not* mechanical in the way we use our brains

intellect: stored knowledge, information-processing, consciousness with all its content—physical, mechanical thought

cognition: the process of understanding based on both intellect and intelligence, on both knowledge and insight into that knowledge—mind and thought working together

Is Your Information All You Are?

If your entire neural circuitry, the whole network of all your life's information in your brain, were downloaded into a huge computer program, would that computer then be you?

There are, it seems to me, two reasons why not.

1. **Our capacity for intelligence is not locatable in the brain to be downloaded.** We don't know where life came from or how it came to be, we don't know exactly what intelligence is, where intelligence comes from, exactly where it lives in the brain, or why nerve tissue in the brain produces it at all. That intelligence does happen in our brains is all we know. Every plant and animal has physical awareness and information or it would be dead. But for the first time in evolution, a brain can actually access its own files. Its awareness is like a password to its own

computer files, into its own memory banks, to enable it to analyze its own experiences, play with possible combinations of actions, generate choices, request answers to problems.

2. **In the human brain, our long childhoods and the plasticity of adolescent brains encourages intelligence and observation, experimentation, instead of mere copycat behavior.** As intelligence can't be downloaded, neither can motive or affection. There is freedom in human adolescence to behave differently from the previous generation, renegotiate behavior and transform the mind, thereby transforming and rewiring the brain altogether. And when we transform our brain, we therefore transform our society. Knowing this, let no one push you to set your brain in cement too quickly. Be unsafe. Be insecure and unsettled down. Be unset in your ways as long as you can. Don't sign the contract you were born with.

The Cosmos Itself May Be the Origin of Intelligence

I agree with the view that intelligence, insight, mind as distinguished from just brains, comes from the fact that every atom, every molecule, every field, every cell, everything in the universe contains intelligence. It isn't, as far as I can tell, a question of finding intelligence here or there or somewhere else. Intelligence is everywhere, in everything.

You can discover this for yourself: using your brain as a receptor, like a satellite dish, let thought's chatter fade into silence. You'll find that time stops, and without time and thought, fear stops. In the absence of thought, which is the past and all past experience, there is fresh insight, which is intelligence, which is the connections of our atoms to all the atoms of the universe. It is an affectionate state, a state of seeing 'all,' not just the separate and limited state of 'me.'

Major Differences between Computers and Human Consciousness

While it is true there are similarities of what-you-program-in-is-what-you-get-out (one with patterns of charges in silicon, the other firings in sets of neurons), there are some major differences between computers and brains.

1. Nothing in a computer understands itself or the world outside itself as we do.

2. Robots might some day be programmed to make little robots, but our definition of life is cellular reproduction, not manufacture.

3. Computers do not seem to have the desire to build better computers as we do.

4. The 'homunculi' or 'selfs' in machines are nonintelligent, discrete, mechanical executors of tasks required electroni-

cally to say 'yes' or 'no'—our brains sum up the system's entire information to perform a task or make a decision.

5. Finally, and perhaps most important, the computer can only respond to memory from past input and programmed information. Human intelligence has the capacity to free itself from past information, be sensitive to new, instant information, and respond not from the past, but with fresh insight, watchful to new outer as well as inner information.

We can and will probably program computers to take over much of the work of the world and future discoveries in outer space. But computers cannot, without human brains to reprogram them, change themselves in any meaningful way. "The human brain's great survival tool, adaptability, is flexible, instantaneous, and, among the best people, ethical. Because these qualities are only available in the instant of facing any challenge from the external world, they cannot be preprogrammed," as we mentioned in *In and Out of Your Mind, Teen Science: Human Bites*.

Rewiring and Transformation

It is this quality of intelligence, insight into thousands of generations of human conditioning that can rewire the brain: just really see this, the generational programming, and then you can decide what is useful and what is destructive.

But even if we see it, and still can't wipe out thousands of years of image-making and fears and fear-based violence, we can at least not act on it. We can change our responses and behavior—and this change of response/behavior will alter the neuronal structure of our brains and lay new behavioral responses that are cooperative, not destructive. We can do this.

The universe is a violent place. Life itself is a triumph. Human beings are among life's and the universe's survivors. We are in the middle of the sixth extinction of most species of life on our own planet right now. After an extinction, evolution goes into overdrive. The Earth and life will go on—with us or without us. Like all animals, plants, bacteria, we have fought for survival, exploiting each other in the fight to get and stay ahead. But fighting for survival must now mean cooperation with life, not killing off whatever comes into focus.

Human beings will survive only if we use our brains, our primary survival tool, to sense and remain in harmony with the purposes of the universe. This is mind over thought, awareness over mechanical reaction, intelligence over knowledge.

SECTION THREE

Brains and Behavior:
The Science of Change

CHAPTER TWELVE

Intelligence Affects Your Conditioning

The Developing Teen Self Is not Set in Cement—
What You Don't Like, Rewire

The Developing Teen

Upside: if you don't like what you are, you can change it.

Downside: no one can do this for you, not teachers, parents, therapists, gurus, girlfriends, boyfriends, books—not even this book. Lots of people, therapies, seminars, books, gurus, teachers, parents, all can point the way. But only you can take the torch and light your own fire. The great fantasy of us all, from childhood to death, is that rescue might be just around the next corner. If other people could change us, surely by now, Jesus and Buddha, Lao Tzu and Mother Teresa would have done the trick.

We've been talking about this throughout the book, so it's no news that the brain cell circuitry is either reinforced or it changes every time you spend another Saturday in front of the television set or yell at your brother—or, conversely, practice a skill, like throwing a ball or writing an essay or restraining yourself from yelling at your brother.

In all the five developmental stages in the human life-span—infancy, childhood, adolescence, adult, old age—development, as Restak says, is a two-edged sword. Development can lead to happiness and skill in living your life, or, if the developmental sequences go wrong, to prolonging the most common horrors of the teen years and often beyond: the three D's, depression, drugs, drinking, and the habit of escaping rather than understanding problems. People who escape problems get stuck in stupid; people who learn to understand their problems move on. While a lot of being in your teens is good, fun, exciting, another part of it is pure torture, outer conflict, inner chaos, loneliness, and total confusion.

To a large extent, there is not much you can do to hurry the maturational process of your frontal lobes. As long as you are in your teens, you are going to be a teenager and that's that. But one of the brain systems that makes us human is our capacity to imagine *future possibilities, if-this-then-that, consequences—even in adolescence.*

Self or LIFE?

A lot is said and written about the importance of developing a *self*, an *identity*. Much of the personal craziness and sorrow in the world is caused by this human habit of wishing, pretending, hoping for a strong, solid, undying, immortal *self.*

We have discovered in the course of this book that self is, quite literally, a figment of thought, a temporary representation of whatever you are feeling, thinking, doing at the moment. A self, such as it is, like a dream, doesn't last. It has passing frames, temporary moods and ideas, an itch on your elbow now, a passion for a boy on a motorcycle later in the afternoon. And if you're alone and drifting, or asleep, or occupied with total interest in something outside you, the self is temporarily suspended. At best, as we've seen, this self thing is gappy, falls apart, spaces out, comes and goes.

You've got a name, of course, so your parents know which kid to pick up from hockey practice if they can't tell or smell you out from a pile of bodies on the ice. But a name is not a self. You can say your name over and over again, and it still does not convince you of an identity. You can win medals, horse races, beauty contests, achievement plaques, honors, a pile of money—it will still not convince you that the you of you is real. Ask any adult you know who is honest, truthful, and intelligent. Until we die, if we really want to waste a lot of time, we pursue the silly illusion that everybody else has a solid self, and there is something wrong with us if we don't. It's the story of *The Emperor's New Clothes* all over again. When the swindlers pretended to make him a suit of gold, his courtiers told him he looked wonderful, and only one little child pointed to him during his parade and said, "But mommy, he's naked."

That's us. Our parents, our culture, our use and construction of language, all convince us we have a self. Organized religion adds that this self or soul is immortal. So we spend our lives feeling left out, lonely, and inadequate, entering every contest and marathon we can find trying to prove we not only have a self but that it will live forever and is a superior self indeed.

Have you ever heard that it isn't choices, it isn't looking for freedom somewhere or somehow, but that it is *the truth that will set you free?*

Be free. Forget about trying to chisel a marble sculpture out of some imaginary self that will last as a monument forever. (You might well remember Ray Fisher's truth about marble monuments: they sit on pedestals in the park, all alone with birds relieving themselves on their heads.)

A better use of your time is to forget about your imaginary self and meditate on how to live your life so you can be happy and serviceable and productive.

Knowing How the Brain Temporarily Assembles the 'Self' Over and Over Again Can Teach Us to Beware (Be Aware of) Its Tricks

For purposes of our dialogue, we'll use the word 'self' not as a permanent reality, but as a temporary image of what you are, all your thoughts, feelings, behaviors, right now. 'Right now' is always: 'right now' has had lots of moments in the past; 'right now' will result in your future. "What you are now you will be tomorrow, unless you change it," as Krishnamurti taught teenagers all over the world in the schools he founded.

In *The Synaptic Self: How Our Brains Become Who We Are*, Joseph LeDoux sets forth his seven principles for the formation and presentation of our temporary selves.

Remember that your brain was assembled during childhood by a combination of genetic and environmental influences that made you more like your family than nonfamily. Then your own experiences with the world further influenced your synaptic connections in the multiple neuronal systems in your brain.

Systems that Assemble the Self

1. **Parallel Encoding: Different systems experience the same world.** They encode such experiences as sights, sounds, smells, differently, but a shared culture develops in the brain. The sound of the word 'lasagna' may immediately call up the sights and smells of family dinner. The

smell of a locker room may call up visions and sounds of camaraderie, excitement; a scent may bring a mental picture of a moonlit night with someone's arms around you and the words "I love you." This is your world; you think "I am thinking about this" instead of more accurately stating, "My brain has manifested its parallel encoding."

2. **Parallel Plasticity: In real brains neural networks do not exist in isolation but communicate via synaptic transmission.** This is simply long-distance communications between brain systems. Jacquelyn sees her boyfriend Raja's face: his face is not just the integration of shape, form, and other visual features, but also the integration of all these features with information and experience stored in Jacquelyn's memory (Raja is special), and its significance for her at the moment (his brain and body excite my brain and my body), in the past (we had fun at the party last Saturday), for the future (I want him to invite me to the prom). Jacquelyn's brain is reacting to a stimulus (Raja's face). Her different brain systems are parallel processing reactions to Raja which thought constructs into a temporary self to construct a love story with her imagined 'self' as Raja's heroine.

3. **Chemical Modulators.** Amines like monoamines— Dopamine, Norepinephrine, Epinephrine, Serotonin and Acetylcholine—regulate transmission, plasticity (learning) and maintenance (memory). When these modulators,

mostly produced by brain stem cells but also distributed throughout the brain, are activated, many brain areas are affected, like a firehouse alarm going off. This happens during significant experiences, emotional, unexpected, painful, or otherwise arousing stimuli. These operate in healthy ways in healthy brains: a yacht is about to run over my raft, I better get out of the way. These chemical modulators operate in disordered ways in mental disorders, or even temporarily during times of stress like economic or adolescent depression. "My brain's modulators are working overtime so it's chemically imbalanced," is truer than "I am depressed." Who is I? And is it the same 'I' as before you got the 'F' in chemistry or before the magazine refused to publish your short story?

4. **The Assembly Mechanism.** Regions of the brain called convergence regions, like the medial temporal lobe, coordinate memories from different systems in a way that allows them to be consciously accessible. The hippocampus is a superconvergence zone; it receives inputs from other convergence zones to create memories, thoughts, and information formed by various other brain systems. Your hippocampus functions so automatically you are not aware of its processes and is a big culprit in the magic trick of convincing you that you have a you. When it's really your hippocampus the whole time.

5. **The Loop.** Assembling a self is not only an automatic process of brain regions responding to genes, environment, experience, but those thoughts and memories that create a sense of self in the executive control convergence center, the prefrontal cortex, the working RAM, in turn reaffect the rest of the brain systems. "A thought is embodied as a pattern of synaptic transmissions within a network of brain cells," says LeDoux, and so "the brain activity that is a thought can influence activity in other brain systems involved in perception, motivation, movement, and the like." A new thought, a new insight, can change your brain's activity just as a new activity can change your brain cells.

6. **Emotional States: Key Role in Brain Activity.** The brain has a number of emotion systems, including networks that identify food sources and sexual partners, as well as identifying and defending against danger. This variable 'you' of you has genetic emotions (don't get eaten, find food to eat and a partner to reproduce with, keep breathing), some environmentally trained emotions (it's disgusting to pick your nose six inches away from a loved one, shameful to get caught with your hand in a variety of cookie jars, really lovely to hug and be hugged), some experiential emotions based on whatever you've been through personally that has pleased, scared, confused you. Emotions penetrate many systems of the brain, some re-

maining fixed in the circuitry, some amenable to plasticity (learning, adapting, and change). Childhood abuse can be indelible, devastating: the fear arousal systems of the brain will too easily be activated in the personality. Childhood trust is equally indelible: the future brain will respond to the world in joyful curiosity, a sharing enthusiasm, and affection.

7. **Contradictions in Brain Systems.** The connections between the emotional systems and cognitive systems in the human brain are, to use a scientific term, iffy. Le Doux says this is because our newly evolved cognitive systems, the technological parts of our brains, are not yet integrated into our more primitive brain systems. I personally translate this to mean that we have not much progressed emotionally/psychologically in half a million years whether we can land ourselves on the moon or not. So if we are going to survive, personally and collectively, we really do have to understand that our intelligence and even our intellectual assessment based in the frontal lobes must be in charge of the more primitive brain systems or our animal terror/aggression combined with our clever technology will surely destroy us.

Clearly the human species is a shared heritage, a shared personality with a few superficial, experiential differences, but the same in basic brain functions. What we call the self is the current, temporary sum of our synaptic connections, our brain's circuitry. The self is not a solid, enduring entity nor is its formation particularly personal or very different from anyone else's.

So, the bad news is the 'you' of you ain't so much, ain't hardly even there except as an idea from moment to moment.

The good news is that, since it isn't a big deal, you can at long last, and despite all the self-help books (this book is emphatically NOT one of them), stop working on your self as if it were, as aforesaid, some marble monument for posterity.

There is work to be done and it's vitally necessary. But not on your so-temporary, illusory 'self,' with all its thoughts and opinions. The work is on your behavior, which begins with understanding your behavior, keeping what you like, and changing the rest.

CHAPTER THIRTEEN

Tools For Change: Self-Knowledge Changes Behavior

Trick or Treat

The self may be a trick played on us by our brains to give us a sense of security and continuity, but it's a powerful trick. After all, it's the brain's job to keep the body alive, and one of the ways it does that is to provide in our species a sense of self, not just an instinct for survival, but a whole scenario of self-importance. But there is a negative side to this trick: self-importance betrays the importance of community, and without community there is no way for naked apes, as Desmond Morris calls us, to survive.

The way to cope with a trick is to understand it, so you control the trick instead of the trick controlling you. The self does not have to be an unexploded bomb going off unexpectedly in your own face and everybody else's. After all, as the Dalai Lama says, the point of life is to be happy.

Understanding the Tricks of the Self

People are always going on about understanding yourself, but they never seem to give you any hints or tools about how to go about this. After years of meetings, reading, traveling, dialoguing, and experimentation, the following tools have proved helpful. Choose ways that suit you, that are comfortable for you. What is important is to have inward silence, silence of the mind, inner space so you can listen to yourself, the many voices of your self collected from all the ages you have ever been. *You don't want to think more thoughts—you want to listen to the thoughts you are thinking.*

The Written Inventory

All you need is a quiet place, a pad or notebook, and a pencil. You don't exist in a vacuum, and to know about yourself is to know yourself in relationship to people, places, things, activities. You won't need paragraphs, this is not a book you're writing, just lists.

On the first page, list your life's people first: mother; father; any important other family members like a grandparent you have strong good or bad feelings about; all your siblings; at least one important friend; one important love-mate; one teacher; one boss. You don't need more—you'll discover your personal characteristics don't change much from person to person. You are passive or possessive, needy or giving, whatever you are with pretty much everybody. The sum of 'you' just works better with some people than others, and we call that a 'good' relationship. Also on this first page, make a list of your places: home, school, church or temple (whether you go or not), sports field, parties or dances or raves or clubs. Make a list of things you use: television, computer, car, telephone, money, whatever. Not a long list, just some. Make a list of your usual activities, important ones like eating food, clothes-shopping, television-watching, sports, studying, chores at home, listening to music.

Relationships

On the next page, start with the first person on your list, for instance, your mother. At the top of the page, write the word 'mother.' You don't need paragraphs here, just number one to five and use just a few words. First write five things you don't like about your mother, then write five things you do about it, or how you react to her. Like: 1) I don't like my mother because she's too angry: what I do about it is escape by leaving the house, or I get angry back at her, or I take it out on my siblings and friends, or I stuff my feelings with food and shopping. 2) I don't like my father because he's too passive during my mother's yelling or stonewalling: what I do about it is tell him to yell back at my mother, or I feel sorry for him and take his side—or whatever. You get the idea.

We have many of our strongest feelings for our families, but the love part doesn't need examination. Loving always works just fine. It isn't love that gets us into trouble. Other emotions do, which is why they need attention. But in this inventory, it is less interesting why you don't like someone or why you get upset at them than what you do about your bad feelings. *You get to know yourself, not by analyzing someone else's defects, but by understanding what you do about what happens to you in life.* Do you run? Escape into food, drugs, drinking, sex, depression? Do you confront? Get angry back? Are you passive-aggressive and save resentments, sulk? Do you punish yourself? Do you try harder, compete?

Examine all your relationships in this manner, not only to people but to places you have to be, things you have to do, to God, to work (school), to money. Writing a quick inventory of your reactions and reactive behaviors is a tool that can help you understand the ways of your 'self' all your life. Sometimes you may need a whole life inventory; sometimes just a quick inventory on a boyfriend or girlfriend or teacher to figure out what you don't like, what you do about it, and whether you want to change your behavior for a better outcome.

It really is interesting to discover how similarly we behave with just about everybody, and how some people like us for exactly the same characteristics that put other people off. You just aren't everyone's favorite person in the world, any more than everyone you know is your favorite person in the world.

Silent Sitting

For some people, sitting is easier than writing.

You don't have to do anything or go anywhere except inside yourself to find out about you. You just have to find a quiet corner somewhere, in your room, under a tree, on a stoop, beach, the floor of a car. Doesn't matter. Sit with your back straight so the lungs in your chest have room to breathe and lower your eyelids so you are not distracted by the outside world. Take a couple of slow, deep breaths.

NOW SIT STILL AND SHUT UP.

That's the whole secret. But sitting still, silently, for even five minutes and doing absolutely nothing in our busy-driven society is not something children are taught to do, so don't push yourself at the beginning. If two minutes is all you can do on the first try, good. You'll get better at it. What you want to do is give your mind the space, time, and quiet to listen to the details of your life. In the quiet, that's the thing: just listen, don't talk back to yourself. At first, your brain, not used to quiet and only used to lists and challenges, will make you crazy with thoughts like:

- What time is the English test tomorrow?

- Want to smack boyfriend for flirting with girlfriend at party last night

- I'm bored—why was I sitting here again?

- Forgot to put hockey uniform in laundry

- Does she like sex or is she just trying to please me?

- Will I be invited to Saturday's party, pass exams, get new thing I wanted?

Some trains of thought that will pass through your brain at first can be funny, or frightening, some may be deep, some trivial. All these thoughts are yours, are you. Whether childhood nightmare memories or ringing ears or movies or the universe—all of this is you. Nothing in there is coming at you from outside.

Make friends with all of it. It's recorded in your brain.

Do this for just a few minutes every day for a week, a month, for the rest of your life if you can, and you will hear what is going on for you and not be suddenly shocked or surprised by what you say and do. You'll know yourself pretty well in this silence—*you'll hear what you are thinking, which is more than most people ever do.* It's the best way in the world to know yourself—to see what's on your mind. Not get involved with it, not argue back with it, just see it. What's going on with you will become clear. And this self-knowledge is the key to freedom from the suffering the self causes. Attention, it turns out, not control, is the way to change one's life.

As you get more practiced, you can bring any problem to your meditation. (Meditation simply means, from the Latin, to pay attention: it has nothing to do with standing on your head in a corner making strange noises in foreign tongues.) You bring a problem into your silence not to think about or analyze. You can just drop it into your silence, like a quarter in a slot, and *listen for, not think about, the answer.* You can find out what interests you to do with your life, what to know about anger or fear, how to handle situations, by asking the universe a question, and in your altered state of consciousness which is your silence, learn the art of listening for what comes to you.

Other people have been doing this for thousands of years. It works. For teachers, books, resources, and further ways into meditation and insight, see *Stop the Pain: Teen Meditations*, in this series of books on living for teens.

Paying Attention in Your Daily Life

Some people who won't write, who can't sit still—and males during their hormone-driven teens may have this difficulty—can learn about themselves another way. Those of you who have difficulty in being still can simply walk around your daily life paying complete, mindful attention to everything you are doing, thinking, feeling. If your own life and what you do every day doesn't happen to you, doesn't interest you, what will?

We live so much of our lives mechanically. There's the experience we've all had of walking or riding somewhere and arriving without knowing how the time passed. It went by without our being conscious of it. Do you really want to arrive on your deathbed, look back at your life, and say, "What was that?"

Eat mindfully (you'll learn things about yourself, like what you really like to eat, whether you really are hungry or whether you're eating out of habit). Think mindfully (you'll learn whether you really hate the people you hate or you've just been taught to distrust them). Walk mindfully (you'll find out whether you even like to walk and whether you're seeing the beauty of the world or just the insides of your own head). Surf, skate, play ball, bike, dance, sing, commune with nature and one another mindfully. Lie down, get up, speak mindfully. Listen to your own opinions, what you like, what you don't like. Experiment with not having opinions all the time, experiment with not even needing to think all the time unless thought is necessary to get across the street. It's very difficult not to like this, dislike that, want this, not want that. Try attention instead of thought, like turning your eyes into windows instead of mirrors. Look at the sky, a tree, a passing face. Really look. Pay full attention to what you are doing, whenever you can. At least call yourself back when your attention wanders, because no one can pay attention all the time. Attention, being there for as many moments of your life as you can manage, will make your life more real, more meaningful, and you'll get to know yourself as your best friend much better. The best friend part is because, while you can't shape anybody else up, you can turn yourself into the best friend you'll ever have. Besides, you are always there.

Whether walking, eating, reading, thinking, moving, or sitting, simply be aware that walking, eating, reading, thinking, moving, or sitting is happening.

Life and Freedom

Freedom is about self-examination, clarity, knowing the truth about yourself, keeping what you like in the contents of your brain, recording over what you don't like. Freedom has nothing to do with life 'choices': choices (we obviously choose a green or blue sweater, this or that car) are made only in a state of confusion. When you have clarity, you know what to do, what personal decisions to make to live your life without harm to yourself or anyone else, what interests you to do in work, in relationship, what you love to do with your time.

As for group decisions, again it is not a matter of choosing your opinion or mine, or everyone contributing lots of different personal opinions based on conflicting selves and their conditioned brain programs. Group decisions must be based on what is good for everyone through the process of a dialogue that arrives at group insight.

Don't live a life, your own, your community's life, according to tape-recorded announcements, digitally programmed software based on all the mistakes of previous generations who still think going to war can make peace.

We have not been a happy species. You can start the human race all over again—and this time, win joy instead of just more of the same old aches and pains.

"To do this, though, we must cooperate with nature," says philosopher Kishore Khairnar, "and use the intellects nature gave us to understand the difference between stale thought and new insight, so we can transform our brains, mutate, and finally evolve psychologically."

Truth, God, and Death

These three, if you ponder them, are really all the same. The truth is, as we've discovered, that the self, all that living according to a past downloaded into our circuits, to blindly obeyed tradition, like a mechanical robot repeating itself over and over whatever it's been taught—this combination of brain circuits that tricks us into thinking we have a self—this is the problem.

As you have discovered for yourself, the self comes and goes, and its absence, even for a few seconds, allows new insights, intelligence, truth, connection, love, goodness, to come in. In other words, it's 'you' or life.

The body does not have to die for you to die: that is, your self with all its ideas and opinions, to die. When Jesus said, "Die to be born again," he knew what he was talking about. He may not have meant the death of the body, but the death of the self and its self-importance.

After all, it's only into an empty glass that anything can be poured: love, God, the intelligence of the universe. Make room.

Physical death is only a return of atoms to atoms. It's the 'me' whose death we are afraid of. Why not let it die over and over again, let it die now, for instance, and never be afraid of death again? If your neuronal circuits record this truth you can live free of psychological fear forever. In *The Future of Humanity*, Krishnamurti and Bohm suggest from both the metaphysicist's and physicist's discoveries, that this mutation of the brain's circuits can actually occur. Insight and attention can change destructive conditioning in the brain. This is not only possible psycho-spiritually, but biologically in the very brain cells themselves. If we are willing to give the same energy to life as we do to our other vital interests, we can let go of this pervasively destructive idea: the unconnected self.

> *It is your responsibility, how you live, how you live your daily life. If you want peace in the world, you have to live peacefully, not hating each other, not being envious, not seeking power, not pursuing competition. Because out of that freedom from these, you have love. It is only a mind that is capable of loving that will know what it is to live peacefully.*

— J. Krishnamurti, *What Are You Doing with Your Life?*

Bibliography and Suggested Reading

Many of the scientists whose work is fundamental to understanding what we know—and what we do not yet know—about how the brain works are mentioned in the text. So are many of the philosophers, physicists, and metaphysical teachers.

The works listed here are accessible to anyone, with or without a science background. While some are not written specifically for young adults, they are written for the general audience and very readable, often humorous, and, rather than lecture, provoke thinking on the part of readers. This is particularly true of Stephen Jay Gould, Steven Pinker, and Stephen W. Hawking. I quote also from the 20th-century philosopher J. Krishnamurti, as he has influenced some of our greatest science minds in areas of neuroscience and psychology.

Major sources for facts and statistics in this book, aside from the following texts, were newspapers, journals, magazines, especially *U.S. News & World Report*, *Scientific American*, *National Geographic*, government publications, almanacs, public television specials, documentaries, news broadcasts, and particularly Ted Koppel's *Nightline*.

Many of the books listed have already been mentioned in the text of this book.

Books on Living for Teens

Carlson, Dale and Hannah Carlson, M.Ed., C.R.C. *Where's Your Head? Psychology for Teenagers*. 2nd edition. Madison, CT: Bick Publishing House, 1998. A general introduction for adults and young adults to the structure of personality formation, the meaning of intelligence, the mind, feelings, behaviors, biological and cultural agenda, and how to transform our conditioning and ourselves.

Carlson, Dale. *Stop the Pain: Teen Meditations*. Madison, CT: Bick Publishing House, 1999. Self-knowledge is true meditation: ways to lose the anxiety, hurt, conflict, pain, depression, addictions, loneliness, and to move on.

BIBLIOGRAPHY AND SUGGESTED READING

————.*Who Said What? Philosophy Quotes for Teens*. Madison, CT: Bick Publishing House, 2003. Teen guide to comparing philosophies of the great thinkers of the ages, religious leaders like Jesus and Buddha, philosophers from Socrates to Krishnamurti, scientists like Freud, Einstein, Darwin, Hawking.

————.*In and Out of Your Mind—Teen Science: Human Bites*. Madison, CT: Bick Publishing House, 2002. Teen guide to all fields of modern science and their ethical use: origin of life and the universe, anthropology and evolution, intellect and intelligence, medical science and genomics.

Krishnamurti, J. *What Are You Doing with Your Life? Books on Living for Teens*. Ojai, California: Krishnamurti Foundation of America, 2001. Understanding how the human brain and mind, intellect and intelligence work so that your brain's self-knowledge will guide your life and actions, not the past with all its mistakes, and not outside authority either to be responsible for you or for your problems.

For further reading on how the mind and brain work, the psychology of human beings and their behavior, you might read what the great philosophers have written in earlier centuries. Their observations were no less acute without technology because of their capacity for objective understanding. The teachings of the Vedas, Krishna, Buddha, Lao Tzu, Confucius, Moses, Jesus, Mohammed, and, in this century, Mother Teresa, the Dalai Lama, and J. Krishnamurti are astute, and, by today's neuroscientific methods, quite accurate. A good source for teens in comparative philosophy is Carlson's *Who Said What? Philosophy Quotes for Teens.*

General

Carlson, Hannah, M.Ed., C.R.C. *Living with Disabilities.* 2nd edition. Madison, CT: Bick Publishing House, 1997. A 6-volume compendium with sections that describe symptoms, origins, treatments for mental disorders, learning disabilities, brain defects and injuries. Includes: *I Have a Friend with Mental Illness.* Also, *The Courage to Lead: Start Your Own Support Group, Mental Illnesses and Addictions.* Madison, CT: Bick Publishing House, 2001.

Dennett, Daniel C. *Consciousness Explained.* Boston: Little, Brown and Co., 1991. Full-scale exploration of human consciousness, informed by the fields of neuroscience, psychology, and artificial intelligence, this is a funny, clear understanding of the human mind-brain. Not easy reading, but worth it.

BIBLIOGRAPHY AND SUGGESTED READING

Gleick, James, editor. *The Best American Science Writing 2000*. New York: HarperCollins, 2000. Science writers and reporters cover their beat as thoroughly as crime, politics, celebrities are covered. Modern life demands we know about the mapping of DNA, about cloning, robotic AI, brain scanning. A variety of articles culled from the best writers and the best magazines.

Gould, Stephen Jay, Ph.D. *The Mismeasure of Man*. New York: W.W. Norton, 1996. Evolutionary biologist Gould's challenge to the hereditary I.Q. as a measure of intelligence and destiny.

————.*Full House*. New York: Three Rivers Press, 1996. Humans are a twig on the bush of life, not the star on top of the tree. A funny, funny man, scientist, writer.

Hawking, Stephen W., Ph.D. *A Brief History of Time: From the Big Bang to Black Holes*. New York: Bantam Books, 1988. A brief, popular, nonmathematical introduction, in words not equations, to astrophysics, the nature and origin of time and the universe. Hawking shows us how our 'world picture' evolved from Aristotle through Galileo and Newton to Einstein and Bohm (relativity and quantum physics—how we affect what we observe).

BIBLIOGRAPHY AND SUGGESTED READING

Horgan, John. *The Undiscovered Mind*. New York: Simon & Schuster, 1999. How the human brain defies replication, medication, and explanation. Science writer examines laboratories, hospitals, the work of neuroscientists, behavioral geneticists, artificial intelligence engineers, consciousness philosophers and analysts to explore the gap between body and mind. Neuroscientists can break the brain to pieces, but they can't put it together again.

J. Krishnamurti. *Education and the Significance of Life*. New York: HarperCollins, 1953. This influential philosopher founded schools in the United States, England, India, and here discusses the purpose of education, the difference between intelligence and intellect, brain and mind, the awakening of a new mind that continues to learn and inquire with both the scientific and religious/philosophy attitudes so that knowledge and our brains will not destroy us.

LeDoux, Joseph, Ph.D. *Synaptic Self: How Our Brains Become Who We Are*. New York: Viking, 2002. The chemical and electrical connections between brain cells provide the biological base for memory, which makes possible the sense of continuity that creates the 'self'. The brain is physical, thought is physical, thought invents the self which is therefore physical, not some 'ghost in the machine' or some little mini-me in the head. Not an easy book to read, but well worth the time and trouble.

BIBLIOGRAPHY AND SUGGESTED READING

Pinker, Steven, Ph.D. *How the Mind Works*. New York: W.W. Norton, 1997. A long but witty, clear, and accessible read by a world expert in cognitive science. Pinker explains what the mind is, how the brain works, how it evolved, how it sees, thinks, feels, enjoys the arts, and ponders the mysteries of life. This is an extraordinary picture of human mental life, with insights that range from evolutionary biology to social psychology.

Ratey, John J., M.D. *A User's Guide to the Brain*. New York: Random House, 2002. 'Perception, Attention, and the Four Theaters of the Brain' is the book's subtitle. Perception captures incoming stimuli; attention, consciousness, and cognition process these perceptions; the major brain functions of movement, memory, language, emotion, and social ability work with this information; the result is behavior and identity.

Restak, Richard, M.D. *The Secret Life of the Brain*. Washington, D.C., co-publishers, The Dana Press and Joseph Henry Press, 2001. Companion to the PBS television series, this lavishly illustrated book explores the ages and stages of the human brain's development from infancy to old age and includes mental disorders and learning disabilities.

Brain Science
Web Sites with Links

Type in: Neurobiology, Neuroscience for Teens in a search engine. You will find excellent sites for Brain Science. Here are some of them. (Remember, sites change.)

Brain: the World Inside Your Head
www.pfizer.com/brain/

ThinkQuest
www.thinkquest.org

Explore the Brain and Spinal Cord
faculty.washington.edu/chudler/introb.html

BRAIN SCIENCE WEB SITES WITH LINKS

Enchanted Learning
www.enchantedlearning.com

The Secret Life of the Brain
www.pbs.org/wnet/brain/

Glossary of Science Terms

a priori: Kant pointed out that time and 3-D space are not things (phenomena) but only the way human brains are born hard-wired to process what we see. Bohm added, "the subtle mechanism of knowing the truth does not originate in the brain."

amygdala: Brain structure of the limbic system responsible for our emotional responses to sensory input.

anthropic principle: We see the universe the way it is because if it were different, we would not be here to observe it.

anthropology: Science of the study of humans, their origin, nature, distribution, characteristics.

artificial intelligence: Computer simulation of human cognitive processes.

atom: The basic unit of ordinary matter, consisting of a tiny nucleus (made up of protons and neutrons) and electrons that orbit around the nucleus.

attention deficit disorder—ADD: Learning disability with impaired capacity to focus attention: distractibility, impulsivity, restlessness—marked by the discrepancy between intellectual capacity to learn and actual performance.

axon: Nerve cell fiber that sends information.

behavior: Anything that an organism does involving action and response to stimuli.

big bang: The explosion of a fiery ball 15 billion or so years ago that contained all matter in the universe and probably even the laws governing it—most cosmologists agree it marks the beginning of the universe and time as we know it, where everything, including us, began.

brain: Brains are, essentially, recording and anticipation machines whose major function is to keep the organism alive in the environment. The brain is the primary center for regulating and coordinating body activities.

GLOSSARY OF SCIENCE TERMS

Broca's area: Crucial center for language and speech, located in a small patch of cortex on the left side of the brain.

cerebellum: The brain mass that lies in the back of the head underneath the cerebral cortex.

cerebrum: Largest part of the brain, consisting of two hemispheres connected by the corpus callosum. The surface folds, called gyri, are separated by fissures.

chromosomes: The long strands of hereditary material composed of nucleic acids that contain the genes.

cognition: The act or process of knowing based on both intellect and intelligence.

conditioning: All the contents of consciousness, ideas, beliefs, reactions, behavioral patterns, everything learned throughout evolution: biological, species, gender, cultural, personal experiences and adaptations; stored information from all time through yesterday.

consciousness: Physical effects of the brain's activities, still very much a mystery to neuroscientists, evolutionary biologists and psychologists, artificial intelligence engineers, neuroanatomists, physicists, metaphysicists, sociologists, behavioral geneticists, to say nothing of philosophers and metaphysicists. Francis Crick once said that consciousness is "attention times working memory." Krishnamurti said, "Consciousness is its contents."

cortex: The large outer layer of the cerebral hemispheres, in major part responsible for our characteristically human behaviors.

cosmology: The study of the universe as a whole.

cyborg: Part of the computer/electronics/robotics world: a human being linked to mechanical/electronic/computer device on which physical systems may depend.

dendrite: Branching fiber that conducts impulses toward the body of a nerve cell.

depression: Mental disorder marked by sadness, dejection, inactivity, difficulty in thinking and concentration, caused by chemical imbalances in the brain usually involving serotonin levels.

DNA: Deoxyribonucleic acid is the genetic material of all life on Earth, consisting of ladder-like sequences of units called nucleotides, usually arranged in a double helix. There are two main types of nucleic acids, DNA and RNA, ribonucleic acid.

entropy: The degradation of matter and energy in the universe to an ultimate standstill.

evolutionary biology: The study of our physical development and change over time.

evolutionary psychology: The study of changes in brain/behavior over time.

field: A field exists throughout space and time, as opposed to a particle that exists at only one point at a time.

four forces: We (not the universe) have grouped force-carrying matter in four categories according to the strength of the force they carry. Ultimately, physicists hope to find a unified theory that will explain all four forces as different aspects of a single force. The four categories of force are: gravitational force, a universal force of attraction according to mass or energy; electromagnetic force which acts with electrically charged particles but not uncharged particles; weak nuclear force which is responsible for radioactivity; strong nuclear force, which holds the quarks together in the proton and neutron, and the protons and neutrons together in the nucleus of an atom.

frontal lobes: The frontal lobes of the cortex are involved in judgement, planning, and sequencing of behavior.

gametes: Mature sperm or egg cells capable of participating in fertilization. Each gamete has 23 chromosomes, half the number of the 46 in an ordinary body or cell.

general relativity: Einstein's theory that the laws of science should be the same for all observers, no matter how they are moving.

genes: Genes control the transmission of hereditary characteristics.

hippocampus: Area of the brain crucial to memory.

hominid: Bipedal primate comprising recent humans and immediate ancestors.

hypothalamus: Brain's hormonal center.

intellect: Knowledge, information-processing, consciousness. Some centers can be found in the brain through MRI.

intelligence: Mind, awareness, insight, perception, understanding, the seats of which cannot be found in scanning the physical brain.

learning: To gain knowledge of, understanding, skill, an ongoing process: a modification of behavior through experience or insight.

limbic systems: The structures of the forebrain under the cortex that are concerned with emotion and motivation, such as the hypothalamus, the hippocampus, and the amygdala.

mass: The quantity of matter in a body, its resistance to acceleration.

meme: A cultural group of ideas that form themselves into distinct units—for example, wheel, jazz, wearing clothes.

memory: Stored learning and experience in the neuronal circuits of the brain and the neural circuitry of the body.

metabolism: The process by which material is converted to energy for vital activities.

metaphysics: Insight into what underlies and goes beyond what we perceive as the physical world.

mind: Found nowhere physically in the brain, mind, being intelligence itself, may have its origin in the universe itself.

monoamines: These function importantly in neural transmissions.

MRI: Magnetic Resonance Imaging is used to scan and observe what parts of the brain are used while a person performs different tasks.

mutation: Inheritable changes in structure and process.

natural selection: Adaptation to changing local environments; adaptive heredity is passing on those traits best suited to the survival of the species.

neuron: Nerve cell. Neurons have three basic parts: the cell body and two nerve fibers called axons and dendrites. The cell body contains genetic materials, proteins to make long- and short-term memory. Glutamate, calcium, enzymes called protein kinases have tasks in brain chemistry needed for learning, forming circuits.

neuroscience: Study of the brain and the physiological links between brain, mind, behavior.

neurotransmitters: Nerve call chemicals that transmit neuronal information across a synapse, the space between nerve cells.

PET scan: Positron Emission Tomography—functional imaging of brain activity. See also: MRI.

phenomena: An observable object, fact, event, scientifically describable and known through the senses rather than through thought.

pongid: Humanlike ape, our near relative.

prefrontal cortex: Area of the brain where executive functions like planning and judgement take place; the site of short-term or working memory and higher order cognition.

schizophrenia: Loss of contact with reality and the experience of delusions and hallucinations.

self: Nonlocatable in the brain, self is not a fixed entity, but invented by thought to give a sense of continuity: it is actually the temporary sum collection of thoughts based on memory scattered all over the brain.

GLOSSARY OF SCIENCE TERMS

synapse: The space between neurons.

thought: Reasoning power based on memory.

weight: The force exerted on a body by a gravitational field.

zygote: A fertilized egg.

Index

A

A priori 200
A User's Guide to the Brain 42
Aborigines 154
Abuse 31, 93, 96, 107, 108,
  109, 112, 178
Adaptation 55, 60, 65, 140,
  152, 202, 206
Addiction 9, 29, 31, 33, 41, 42,
  106, 109, 110, 112, 192, 194
  alcohol 12, 13, 30, 34, 77,
  103, 106, 109, 110
  drugs 42, 77, 109, 110, 112
Addictive, mood-altering
  drugs 33, 34, 109

Adolescence 28, 73, 96, 103,
  105, 117, 129, 165, 171, 172
Adulthood 76, 96, 129
Africa 61, 93, 135, 141, 144,
  145, 146, 150, 153, 154, 155
AIDS 108
Alcoholics Anonymous 129
Alcoholism 12, 13, 30, 34, 77,
  103, 106, 109, 110
Alzheimer's disease 112
Amygdala 28, 30, 37, 38, 49,
  94, 103, 106, 132, 163, 205
Ancestors 61, 62, 64, 135, 138,
  141, 144, 146, 148, 153, 154,
  205
Angelou, Maya 52, 90

INDEX

INDEX

D

Dalai Lama 181, 194

Darwin, Charles 63, 64, 65, 119, 137, 139, 140, 193

  natural selection 65, 118, 138, 140, 148, 149, 155, 206

  Origin of Species 64, 137, 139

Death 49, 93, 103, 171, 189, 190

Dementia 130

Dendrite 19, 45, 123, 128, 159, 203, 206

Dennett, Daniel C. 5, 20, 21, 47, 54, 138, 155, 194

Depacote 104

Depression 12, 27- 31, 33, 37, 39, 41, 77, 94, 103, 104, 110, 161, 171, 176, 183, 192, 203

  clinical 31, 37

  manic depression, bipolar disorder 81, 104

  major depression 29, 103

Despair 20, 104

Determinism 140, 155

Developmental stages 39, 56, 171

Disabilities 81, 105, 112, 194, 197

Dissociative amnesia 107

Dissociative disorders 101, 107

Dissociative identity disorder 108

  multiple personality disorder 108

DNA 128, 153, 154, 155, 195, 203

Dopamine 28, 33, 103, 109, 175

Down's Syndrome 112

Dragons of Eden 60, 135

Dreams 33, 55, 98

Drug addiction 42, 77, 109, 110, 112

Drugs 9, 12, 22, 32, 33, 34, 96, 106, 109, 110, 112, 160, 171, 183

  antidepressant 29, 76, 104

  psychoactive 16, 29, 76, 104, 106, 124

Drugs, dealing 32

Dyslexia 32, 67, 68, 70, 71, 74, 75

E

Early Man 142

Education 17, 30, 39, 56, 67, 68, 71, 73, 80, 119, 196

Education and the Significance of Life 80

Einstein, Albert 155, 195, 204

  electromagnetic force 204

Emotional centers 29

INDEX

INDEX

INDEX

Old age 56, 130, 171, 197
Oppositional 69
Origin of Species 64, 137, 139

P

Pain xvii, 9, 16, 24, 26, 31, 33,
  40, 63, 77, 79, 105, 122, 186,
  192
Panic disorder 37
Parallel encoding 174
Parents 9, 10, 23, 28-30, 32,
  35, 36, 38, 44, 65, 67, 71, 72,
  76, 77, 90-92, 110, 111, 129,
  131, 140, 148, 149, 151, 160,
  170-173
Parkinson's disease 112, 161
Pathological behavior 37
Paxil 29, 104
Peers 8, 30, 32, 35, 36, 40, 70,
  75, 91, 97, 101, 144, 148,
  149, 152, 160, 170, 183
Perception 43, 57, 105, 163,
  164, 177, 197, 205
Personality 4, 13, 19, 21, 23,
  28, 34, 57, 78, 94, 101, 105,
  106, 108, 129-132, 156, 178,
  192
  addict 13, 22, 34, 35
  artist/writer/musician 13,
    43, 84, 85, 87
  genius 90
  impaired 13
  jock 13, 59, 61, 133, 134

mystic 13
nerd 46, 59, 60, 61, 63, 88,
  133, 134
popular/cool 13, 27, 91,
  118, 124, 130
revolutionary 13
romance, sex junkies 13
science and math 13
techie 13
Personality disorders 13, 101,
  105, 108
  borderline personality 105
  obsessive-compulsive
    personality 105
PET scan 207, *see also MRI*
  84, 101, 104, 106, 163
Pharmacology, *see Drugs,*
  Medication
Phenomena 55, 200, 207
Philosophy 9, 24, 40, 136, 137,
  155, 193, 194, 196
Phobias 37, 94, 107, 149
Pinker, Steven 5, 45, 54, 60,
  88, 118, 134, 142, 143, 148,
  150, 158, 159, 191, 197
Plasticity 122, 130, 165, 175,
  178
Plato 159
Pleasure centers 33
Pleasure circuits 34, 109
Pongid 142, 207
Popularity 91, 124, 151
Post-traumatic stress disorder
  (PTSD) 37, 94, 107

INDEX

BICK PUBLISHING HOUSE
PRESENTS
Books for Teenagers
Science & Philosophy

NEW!

THE TEEN BRAIN BOOK Who & What Are You?
by Dale Carlson. Pictures by Carol Nicklaus.
Edited by Nancy Teasdale, B.S. Physics

Understand your own brain, how it works, how you got the way you are, how to rewire yourself, your personality, what makes you suffer

- Who and what are you? The brain's best kept secret!
- Are you really free to choose your life? What is this 'self'? Why do you, your family, your friends behave the way they do?
- The teen brain and how it develops: teen brain circuits, judgement, I.Q., intelligence, sense of responsibility: brain science, neuroscience, for teens
- Are you unique, or like everybody else? Robots, cyborgs, and you! Genes, environment, evolution
- Ages and stages: brains and behavior: talents, mental problems, misfits
- Rewiring by refiring: how to change yourself: tools to change your brain circuits yourself
- How to change what you don't like about yourself, what makes you suffer—teen stories to identify yourself

Author of dozens of books for Young Adults, Carlson has been awarded three ALA Notable Book Awards, the Christopher Award, and is listed on New York Public Library's Best Books for Teens.

The New York Times Book Review says of Carlson, "She writes with "intelligence, spunk and wit."

Publishers Weekly says, "A practical focus on psychological survival."

Illustrations, Index, 256 pages, $14.95.
ISBN: 1-884158-29-3

.

BICK PUBLISHING HOUSE
PRESENTS
Books for Teenagers
Science & Philosophy

Who Said What?
Philosophy Quotes for Teens
by Dale Carlson. Pictures by Carol Nicklaus

Teen guide to comparing philosophies of the great thinkers of the ages: form your own philosophy.

"Thought-provoking guide." —School Library Journal

Illustrations, Index, 256 pages, $14.95.
ISBN: 1-884158-28-5

NEW!

In and Out of Your Mind
Teen Science: Human Bites
By Dale Carlson. Edited by Kishore Khairnar, M.S. Physics

Teens learn about our minds, our bodies, our Earth, the Universe, the new science—in order to make their own decisions. This book makes science fun and attainable.

"Heady stuff." — School Library Journal

Illustrations, Index, 256 Pages, $14.95.
ISBN: 1-884158-27-7

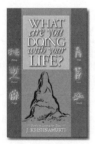

What Are You Doing with Your Life?
Books on Living for Teenagers
By J. Krishnamurti. Edited by Dale Carlson

Teens learn to understand the self, the purpose of life, work, education, relationships.

The Dalai Lama calls Krishnamurti "one of the greatest thinkers of the age." Time magazine named Krishnamurti, along with Mother Teresa, "one of the five saints of the 20th century."

Illustrations, Index, 288 Pages, $14.95.
ISBN: 1-888004-24-X

BICK PUBLISHING HOUSE
PRESENTS
Books for Teenagers
Psychology & Meditation
by Dale Carlson • Hannah Carlson, M.Ed., CRC
NEW EDITIONS

Stop the Pain: Teen Meditations
New York Public Library Books 2000 List
Independent Publishers Award
Teens have their own ability for physical and mental meditation to end psychological pain.

- What Is meditation: many ways
- When, where, with whom to meditate
- National directory of resources, centers

"Much good advice...." — *School Library Journal*

Illustrated, indexed, 224 pages, $14.95;
ISBN: 1-884158-23-4

Where's Your Head? Psychology for Teenagers
New York Public Library Books 2000 List
YA Christopher Award Book

- Behaviors, feelings, personality formation
- Parents, peers, drugs, sex, violence, discrimination, addictions, depression
- Joys of relationship, friends, skills
- Insight, meditation, therapy

"A practical focus on psychological survival skills."
— *Publishers Weekly*

Illustrated, indexed. 320 pages, $14.95;
ISBN: 1-884158-19-6

Girls Are Equal Too: The Teenage Girl's How-to-Survive Book
ALA Notable Book
The female in our society: how to change.

- Girls growing up, in school, with boys
- Sex and relationships
- What to do about men, work, marriage, our culture: the fight for survival.

"Clearly documented approach to cultural sexism."
— *School Library Journal*

Illustrated, indexed, 256 pages, $14.95;
ISBN: 1-884158-18-8

■

BICK PUBLISHING HOUSE
PRESENTS
Books for Health & Recovery

The Courage to Lead—Start Your Own Support Group: Mental Illnesses & Addictions
By Hannah Carlson, M.Ed., C.R.C.

Diagnoses, Treatments, Causes of Mental Disorders, Screening tests, Life Stories, Bibliography, National and Local Resources.

"Invaluable supplement to therapy."
— *Midwest Book Review*

Illustrated, indexed, 192 pages, $14.95;
ISBN: 1-884158-25-0

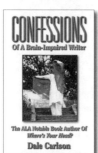

Confessions of a Brain-Impaired Writer
A Memoir by Dale Carlson

"Dale Carlson captures with ferocity the dilemmas experienced by people who have learning disabilities...she exposes the most intimate details of her life....Her gift with words demonstrates how people with social disabilities compensate for struggles with relationships."

— Dr. Kathleen C. Laundy, Psy.D., M.S.W.,
  Yale School of Medicine

224 pages, $14.95, ISBN: 1-884158-24-2

Stop the Pain: Adult Meditations
By Dale Carlson

Discover meditation: you are your own best teacher. How to use meditation to end psychological suffering, depression, anger, past and present hurts, anxiety, loneliness, the daily problems with sex and marriage, relationships, work and money.

"Carlson has drawn together the diverse elements of the mind, the psyche, and the spirit of science...Carlson demystifies meditation using the mirrors of insight and science to reflect what is illusive and beyond words." — R.E. Mark Lee, Director, Krishnamurti Publications America

Illustrations, 288 pages, $14.95;
ISBN: 1-884158-21-8

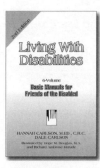
.

■

ORDER FORM

307 NECK ROAD, MADISON, CT 06443
TEL. 203-245-0073 • FAX 203-245-5990
www.bickpubhouse.com

Name: _____

Address: _____

City: _____ State: _____ Zip: _____

Phone: _____ Fax: _____

QTY	BOOK TITLE	PRICE	TOTAL
	YOUNG ADULTS/TEENAGERS		
	The Teen Brain Book	14.95	
	Who Said What? Philosophy Quotes for Teens	14.95	
	In and Out of Your Mind: Teen Science: Human Bites	14.95	
	What Are You Doing with Your Life?	14.95	
	Stop the Pain: Teen Meditations	14.95	
	Where's Your Head?: Psychology for Teenagers	14.95	
	Girls Are Equal Too: The Teenage Girl's How-To-Survive Book	14.95	
	BOOKS FOR HEALTH & RECOVERY		
	The Courage to Lead	14.95	
	Confessions of a Brain-Impaired Writer	14.95	
	Stop the Pain: Adult Meditations	14.95	
	BOOKS ON LIVING WITH DISABILITIES		
	Living with Disabilities	59.70	
	I Have a Friend with Learning Disabilities	9.95	
	I Have a Friend with Mental Illness	9.95	
	BOOKS ON WILDLIFE REHABILITATION		
	Wildlife Care for Birds and Mammals	59.70	
	I Found a Baby Bird, What Do I Do?	9.95	
	I Found a Baby Duck, What Do I Do?	9.95	
	I Found a Baby Opossum, What Do I Do?	9.95	
	I Found a Baby Rabbit, What Do I Do?	9.95	
	I Found a Baby Raccoon, What Do I Do?	9.95	
	I Found a Baby Squirrel, What Do I Do?	9.95	
	First Aid for Wildlife	9.95	
	TOTAL		
	SHIPPING & HANDLING: $4.00 (1 Book), $6.00 (2), $8.00 (3-10)		
	AMOUNT ENCLOSED		

Send check or money order to Bick Publishing House. Include shipping and handling.
**Also Available at your local bookstore from: BookWorld,
Baker & Taylor Book Company, and Ingram Book Company**

■

Author

 *Dale Carlson*
Author of over fifty books, adult and juvenile, fiction and nonfiction, Carlson has received three ALA Notable Book Awards, and the Christopher Award. She writes novels and nonfiction books for young adults, and general adult nonfiction. Among her titles are *The Mountain of Truth* (ALA Notable Book), *Girls Are Equal Too* (ALA Notable Book), *Where's Your Head?: Psychology for Teenagers* (Christopher Award, New York Public Library Best Books List), *Stop the Pain: Teen Meditations* (New York Public Library Best Books List), *In and Out of Your Mind: Teen Science* (New York Public Library Best Books List), *Wildlife Care for Birds and Mammals. Stop the Pain: Adult Meditations* follows her teen meditation book. Carlson has lived and taught in the Far East: India, Indonesia, China, Japan. She teaches writing here and abroad during part of each year. She makes her home among her grandchildren Chaney, Jacquelyn, Malcolm, Sam, and Shannon, and her cats in Connecticut.

■

Editor

Nancy Teasdale, B.S. Physics
Scientist and award-winning dramatist, with a degree from Worcester Polytech Institute, Teasdale migrated from relativity and cosmology to the more immediately practical fields of manufacturing engineering for computer chips and supply chain management for peripherals. She is also an experienced science writing editor and is currently the Senior Science Editor for Bick Publishing House. She makes her home in Massachusetts with her husband and two sons.

Illustrator

Carol Nicklaus
Known as a character illustrator, her work has been featured in *The New York Times*, *Publishers Weekly*, *Good Housekeeping*, and *Mademoiselle*. To date she has done 150 books for Random House, Golden Press, Atheneum, Dutton, Scholastic, and more. She has won awards from ALA, the Christophers, and The American Institute of Graphic Arts.

.

Notes

Notes

Notes

Notes

Notes

Notes

Notes